The Truth About These Three

The Home, the School, and the Church

by

Reverend Ivy Williams, BTH, MRE

DORRANCE PUBLISHING CO., INC.
PITTSBURGH, PENNSYLVANIA 15222

For information or to order additional books, please write:
Dorrance Publishing Co., Inc.
643 Smithfield Street
Pittsburgh, Pennsylvania 15222
U.S.A.

DEDICATION

This book is dedicated to my lovely wife Evelyn (Evy) Williams, my daughter, Tonish Oran Elmore, and my granddaughter Victoria (Lady) Morgan, who have been great assets and supporters of this book.

May God continue to bless each of you.

CONTENTS

PREFACE

Each of us as an individual is responsible for the world in which we live for the peace, safety and well being of each other. God gave us the world, and He gave us the opportunity to make the world what He would have it to be. Unfortunately we have different ideas. In our situation today, we live in a world filled with sorrow, bloodshed, hatred, racism, and all of the things throughout the nation that have contaminated the glory of God simply because the greatest three institutions that God put in the lives of the human family have broken communication and lost fellowship with each other. When the home becomes broken, it automatically brings a breakdown to the other two—the school and the church. The problem is getting worse instead of better. There's no way you can fix the home in other places; home issues will have to be corrected in the home. Nothing else can undo what has been done. When the home becomes broken, it is unable to bring forth the fruit to the school and the Church, which means the entire world is affected.

We have today new trouble, new kinds of incidents. When you think you have heard the worst, the next day you hear something, and it makes the other seems like nothing. Until the correction is made in the home, there is no way we can overcome the non productive elements in the home, the school, and the Church.

When you think of the people, the head of these institutions, the parents are the victims, the teacher is handicapped, and the minister is overloaded with programs for entertainment. Ninety-eight percent of these programs are nonessential to salvation—all because of the breakdown of these three: the home, the school, and the Church.

INTRODUCTION

This book concerns the home, the school, and the Church and has been written to verify or to declare the Church to many people today and to define the Church. What is the Church? And who makes up the Church? What is the Church like when we look at the world in which we live? We are carried away with the organization of the Church. Many, many people try to live a spiritual life, and they claim their belief in the Church, their knowledge of it, and their participation in it, which is the organization of the Church. They know nothing about it as an *organism*.

No one is teaching anything concerning the *organism*, which is the Church—the New Testament Church. The Church is not a building. The Church is built by the Lord Jesus himself, and it is not a building constructed with mortar and brick. It's not built with material things.

Many times the statement is made throughout the land that there is no perfect Church. The New Testament Church of Jesus Christ is a perfect Church, because the Church consists of Him. The Church, to us, is invisible; it is beyond division. But it is much present in power. It's invisible power.

The Church is the body of the Lord and Savior Jesus Christ. The only way we can become a member of that Church is to be born into that Church through the Spirit of God. Motions and seconds by people cannot get you into the Church. They do not operate Christ's Church. The government does not operate the Church.

Thank God for this country where Church and state are separate. Many have tried and are still trying to involve the Church with the government for their own gain.

The Church is the Lord Jesus Christ, and the Church is not operating and functioning by and with things. It operates by the Spirit of God only and His power.

rograms. We have used all of the programs
y to make the Church better, and we have
n throughout the world as the Church of the
become more of an entertainment or style
tever you please—because we have tried to build
ie world and in the way the world operates. Every
s brought us to the peak, and we have run out of
titles . . . We have ran out of spiritual consciousness concerning the Cu. ch. The Church is not known to be a place of
worship, but a place of entertainment and rest. You'll find more people asleep in the congregation today than you will find witnessing,
and we don't even disturb them while they are asleep. The ushers will
usher out those who worship too loudly and ignore those who came
to rest and who are sound asleep.

Our preaching has become a notion of entertainment. Most people are not listening for the Word sent from the Lord but only to how
it sounds. If you don't have the sound, melody, or the formality of
hollering and screaming, then you don't have anyone to witness what
you are saying. That's because entertainment is all they expect, and
we have lost sight of the destiny of our Church life.

We don't seem to be interested in the promises of the Lord and
what the reward will be at the final destination if we keep the faith
and do the will of God. We are busy getting our reward by prestige.
Everybody is trying to outdo somebody else. Everybody is trying to
outpreach somebody else. Everybody is trying to outsing somebody
else. None are benefiting, and all of our energy is wasted. We trust
that we will think and reexamine and reiterate our stand as leaders
and followers and think about where we are going.

Can we find something in our destination that is better than the
place from which we have come? If not, we better think now, because
time is running out on us. We seem to be more delighted in where we
came from and where we say we are going. Our preaching has become
so political and so filled with stories it has built up not a spiritual standing but one of popularity. People are losing their spiritual sensibility.
Those who have been trying for many years have lost hope and have
become disinterested in what's going on. Many things are happening
and have happened in our community, because the Church has not
had its chance to do its job in the human family.

Sports have taken over our worship day. Television, stories, and
dreams have robbed us of our time and common sense. We are

blaming each other over nothing. We are hating each other because we don't have the love of God. We have become dangerous to each other. We're in such a predicament there is no rest. We are restless in our own homes. The young people are locked up in jail, and the parents are locked up at home. The bars at the jails are holding the youth confined. The windows and doors are the bars at home which keep the parents locked up. Dope and all kinds of garbage penetrate the mind of the human family. Nobody can help anybody because we have turned from God, set our own standards, and moved the Church out of its organization and delighted in its beauty, and its formalities, and we feel good about it. Evangelism in our Church is dead. Religious training is barely alive. We neglect the Gospel and fill the emptiness with meaningless storytelling. We fill the air with jokes worse than the sense of humor. We are fighting a storm, and we know where it came from. We are planting seeds that will make communities worse than the ones in which we live. We refuse to take time out and seek the answer.

The problem is that communities are not made by schools, strategy, or government. They emerge from the home. The community is made up of the children we have reared. If we want a good community, we have to plant and feed it in the lives of the children. If it doesn't come that way, it is impossible to have. The government is kicked around more than a football. We live in a blessed country, but everyone is crying out and saying that it's the worst, because we don't have time to thank God for what we have already.

We're the leading country for the world of prosperity, peace of mind, and convenience, and we can't see any of it because we are troubled. We just need a little more. We have become so disgusted with even the government, or the mockery that has made this country what it is, until nobody can please us. We send our officials to the White House to carry on the government business as they always have done and to make this country what it is today. Men, women, boys, and girls at home across the country want to tell officials what to do, how to do it, and how to do it best, and when the leadership is broken down, you can't go anywhere. They come up with such silly ideas that when you are blind, the worst looks the best.

Take, for example things like term limits. Term limits have always been in this country. The people have elected some representatives for two years, some for four, and occasionally, some for six. Those elections are term limits. Most people on the outside can always be the best, much better than the ones on the inside. Innocence looks bright to us sometimes, with eight or ten men running for president and trying to convince everyone that they are better than the president who is in the seat. They have never been president, and some have never even been to Washington. It takes just a few words to show how blind and silly we can be when we are blind, not so much physically but in understanding, and fail to be thankful.

Our Lord said to be faithful over a few, and He will add or make you dominion over many. The Church is ineffective in the midst of our people. There are people who are angry in trying to build themselves through their careers or through fooling people. They are going to do something with the prayers in school. The prayers in the schools are not the problem. The people talking about prayer in the schools don't ever go to the prayer house, which is the house of God. They don't pray at home; they don't believe in prayer. But it's something to use as a way to better their own ambition and ego. It's a play. It's playing with life. This world would be a different world, a world that we could live in.

Hate and racism are the worst kinds of filth that can form in the minds of people. To hate people and not even know them can destroy people. We hate them because of the color of their skin. People exalt themselves based on skin color and we don't know of what we really consist. It's not the flesh; it's not our color; it's not our outer appearance, but the contents of our inside. If our heart is not right, color won't correct it. If our mind is warped, nothing can ease that but the settling of the mind, the correction of the mind. Only the Lord can give us true regulation in the mind. Styles and formalities have proudly blocked the church and driven out the spirit, and everyone is blaming everyone else.

There is no reason to blame everyone else, because there is no one doing anything. We have more jewelry in the pulpit than we have messages and lessons. Homosexuals are sweeping the country. Homosexuality is a disgrace to the human family, and some approve of it, and try to do something about it when God has already given them up. Hatred stems from anything we make it to be. We are self-destructive. We are destroying ourselves. We're slowly destroying ourselves unconsciously of with our better to live than die attitudes. It's more profitable to enjoy our living than to suffer forever for eternity.

If we look at the Church as what it is, we seek to be that Church.

Jesus built that Church in the hearts of men. He built it in the hearts of everyone who will believe. He gave the direction of the Church. Jesus didn't let the Church go out into the world until it was well built. Man and his power cannot destroy the Church. The Church is invisible in the hearts of those who are born of it. The Church uses our voice to speak and uses our body for Christ's temple. Christ's teachings becomes our way of life.

We can't live right unless we let the Church direct us. The Church was built to become the life of those who participate in the Church. The same teachings that Jesus gave to us before he built the Church are the same teachings that the Church provides through those who are teaching. The Church regulates and guides us. It disciplines us in a divine way. It teaches us how to be honest on our jobs, with our neighbors, or in our homes. It teaches us how to have compassion for each other, respect for each other, to bear one another's burdens, to show neighborly love to all, and to welcome the opportunity to do good to each other.

These actions are the works of the Church, and when the Church assembles at the house of God, it has a lot for which to worship the Lord and to praise the Lord. And that's where our joy comes from. The people of the Church don't need substitutes.

When the Lord awakens you in the morning, you don't need a cup of coffee to make your day go right. Just think about it. It was the Lord who woke you up. You don't need a cigarette to make your day bright. Just move your arms and limbs and think. You know right from wrong. You know your right foot from your left foot. It is encouraging to know that God is still using you in His world. That's the Church. The house sits where you build it. The building remains until it is torn down. Every time someone is filled with the Holy Spirit, the Church is being built. It grows. Please understand that the Church is not built through you if you do not have a part in the salvation. If you're not seeking others to become an addition to the building of that Church, you are not aware of who you are and what the Church is. The Church is not a maneuvered government, man, style, or tradition. The Church was not born until all of this was taken into consideration and all things were put in their proper prospective by Jesus. Just think of the good things that happened when the Church was born. If the dumb could speak and tell what happened, or the fouls of the air, or the animals, they would tell you that it saved us from contained things. It saved us from dying for our blood, or our blood being sacrificed or tormented. It saved us. It allowed us to live longer, and men could say it allowed us to live forever.

Look at the different world the Church made after it was born. It gave us the privilege to approach the Lord by the name of Jesus and to carry our problems directly to the Lord. We don't have to carry our sins to the priest or anyone else. Wherever the sin is committed, we can go in peace, concentrate, and pray on the spot, and Jesus will forgive us for the sin. We can't afford to live in sin, because we are the Church, and the Church must operate through us. That's why he said in Romans 12:1 "I beseech you therefore, brethren, by the mercies of God, that ye present your bodies a living sacrifice, holy, acceptable unto God, which is your reasonable service." Only God can live in an unclean temple and bring a clean life that is lived every day. He must have full control. You must believe that you can do right. Know that you can practice doing right and if you practice doing right you become good at whatever you want to be. The individual who rehearses long enough, who studies music long enough, will be able to sing. Those who attend school require time, and if they work hard enough they will learn. You will move from an amateur to professional. You'll be good if you practice long enough. If you practice being right, you'll do right. If you go to bed right, you'll wake up right in the morning. If you think right, you're going to strive to accomplish righteousness in your life. So there's no excuse. We are our own trouble simply because we refuse to seek what is right to make us better people.

Even in the community and places where we live, we need each other. We need each other because we're all in the same world. We're responsible for the world in which we live. We owe our neighbors respect. We owe our neighbors courtesy and politeness, and they owe us. We owe each other, and when we pay our debts, it makes a better community. Through the Church, we have to know each other, because we're of one accord, one spirit, one Lord, and one baptism. But, many have wrong conceptions. Let us look at how some have taken advantage of others' ignorance.

We have ministers here today who have used the Church for their own well being. Not too long ago, some of our leading ministers stood up and recognized they were not preaching sound doctrine. Instead of praying to the Lord to repent and to make corrections, they wanted to change the Gospel. They say now they were preaching, full Gospel. Now, in their Bible it also says, "There's but one gospel." It's dangerous to try to preach any other gospel. Galatians 1:8 tells us even if "an angel from heaven preaches any other gospel...let him be accursed." But when we turn from the general principles and truths of God, we become blind to our own ignorance, and we will disgrace ourselves. Many times we might feel badly about it if we succeed in gangs, if we are popular, and other things. But when we think that these things are causes for souls being lost, it uses up time and ideas to reach the unsaved by working tricks and playing games based upon the ignorance of those who claim to be active in the organization. Those who do know not the Lord don't have a chance.

In the Church, in the organization, there's very little that can be accepted by God. We have too many kings, too many chiefs, and not enough indians. Too many people dominate. They want to run the Church and boss the Church. They want to let their own minds and ideas become dominant in the Church. They want to be the preacher. They want to be officers. They want to be four or five people at the same time, and they are unable to be one active and responsible person. This behavior causes a conflict. The Church of the living God, the New Testament Church, doesn't have a chance, because the Church teachings will condemn all of these unfruitful and unspiritual ideas that have been indoctrinated by the Church. The ministers of the Church are treated as some officers from a voter's league or some other organization with some kind of control, bylaws, or constitution.

I will never sign such document in order to stay at a place. I will never take a course from such men. Many of them haven't been born of the Spirit of God. You cannot teach a spiritual lesson if you don't have a spiritual heart. If you're not inspired, if you're not walking in the will of God, you cannot do it. You will fail in trying. The saddest part is that you will go down and carry many with you.

So then, the Church must come alive. The Church must be identified, and we must be born in it for it to take its rightful place where it belongs, which is in the hearts of human beings so that they can dedicate themselves to the will of God. What we like in our schools, homes, governments, states, and communities, the Lord still has. But it can be performed through the Spirit only and the guidance of the Lord himself. The Lord furnishes love. The Lord furnishes wisdom so that we might increase our knowledge and conduct ourselves accordingly to his will. The Lord is the author of good neighborhoods. He has all of them and had hem before He withdrew, because we ran out of people who live according to the spiritual level. We stopped training and disciplining our children.. We have lost control. The courts have taken over the last say about what's best for our children. Foster homes have taken over, and people have made a living seeing after your children.

The elderly people's lives are short because of businesses like nursing homes. They are good places for the people of children who don't have time for their parents. Lock them up, go on, and forget about them. The elderly have been taken out of our lives, and we are deprived of their teaching and experience in our homes and churches. Our schools have become dangerous, and our children have been blocked from learning their rightful place in this society because they failed, or because they were taught hatred, disobedience, and selfishness at home. Parents are contaminating the minds of the children concerning the teachers as they grow up in the homes. The children have to go to the educators for help. When the children get there, they don't know how to receive help from them. The parents have informed them they can have their own way in the classrooms and in the schools.

We found that the greatest problems in the schools are children refusing to follow guidelines, and having a low opinion of education. They would like to reach positions in life, and in the world, but they don't want to go to school. No one has told them education is essential and is the highway to their dreams and accomplishments.

Therefore, when we leave God, we leave the rich issues of life. When we leave the one who has given us life and when we try to do it ourselves, we're headed in the wrong direction and end up with the wrong results. We have to put these things in their proper prospective. We must understand that the Lord giveth, and the Lord taketh away. In a matter of time, everything in this world that belongs to us, someone else will possess, and we will be gone. If we would get wise and smart, we would do our best to make it better for the ones coming after us so that they might do a better job than what we are doing. That is what makes a better world to live, and keeps the fear of the Lord penetrated in the minds of generations to generations. The Lord will never run out of blessings, because he owns everything. He will always fulfill his promises to everyone who believes.

There are three institutions God has established in the lives of the human family. It takes all three, all of them in unity, or the life is not complete. It takes these three in unity to carry out the mission together. These three are the home, the school, and the church.

These three institutions play a major role that completes the life of every individual who is born into this world. You cannot leave one out and have a complete life; it takes all three in time and in their own perspectives. They fit in together and make a good community, good home, good school, good government, and good world. But if any one of the three is left out, there's an emptiness that's left in the individual.

The first is the home. Each of us comes from the home. There are some home basics that must be rendered to every person who is born and grows up in the home. Each must be born accordingly and in the image of the parents. The parents' attitudes and abilities are what they render to the life of that child and what determines the type of child and how that child's future will develop. This development begins early. It begins by practicing and teaching that child. And if the child doesn't get it, there will be a failure in developing that child's mind. From the home, the child is sent to school, and the kind of discipline and attitude that the child brings to school depends upon his or her time to spend in the school.

The most important aspect is shaping the child's future to fit into society, which means the child must have the right attitude, and that comes from respect. If the child doesn't respect his or her parents, the child won't know how to respect anyone else. If the child doesn't know how to talk to or obey his parents, it's impossible for the child to render to respect someone else. If the child has been fed with the wrong things, wrong information concerning those with whom he will be spending his time in school, he will not know how to conduct himself or respect others.

Children should be taught that adults are not their equal playmates, and they should always respect the right instruction from all parents. They must learn this respect at home. If the parents teach hate and demonstrate hate, if the parents teach that some people are better than others, if they teach some people are somebody and others are nobody, they produce the same attitudes from those who come from their homes.

I think your home has a right to stand on its own principles. If you produce that kind of fruit, it should be known so those around you will respect you for who you are. Children must learn how to relate and how to answer to their elders, their teachers, and their ministers. If they don't learn to respect them in their homes where they live, it's impossible for them to automatically know what to do. If a child doesn't know how to give table a grace at home, he or she cannot be expected to do it away from home. If a child doesn't know the mean-ing of the word respect, if the words "Sir," "Yes Sir," and "Thank You," are not used in their proper place, the questions are where is the child going to use it? What's the purpose of it? Why learn it? What are you going to do with it?

The thing today is that the parents and the teachers have no com-munication. The mind of a child reminds you of a computer. You feed it what you want it to store and what you want to come out when you press the button. It's the same thing. When the child goes to school, the teacher has the responsibility of trying to reach what they have in them. Life comes from the inside, and too much comes from the child's inside that the teachers can't handle. They don't have anywhere to place them. They are not experts on what they meet in the classroom. It's ridiculous. Go to school now when class-es change. High school students don't have the intelligence to change classes. They go through the halls like a herd of cattle on a stampede. You would think they were going to tear the building down with their screaming and hollering and beating their hands against the walls. But they didn't learn that behavior in school. They brought it with them from wherever they came. They cannot come to school with wrong things on their minds and be expected to do right.

The parents should teach their children to respect the teacher, because without respect, it's difficult for the teacher to get their attention, which means the children will never learn.

You know what? If you cease to listen, you cease to learn. So it's very important for the parents to renew their relationship and fel-lowship with the teachers because they are a personal part of every child's life. I also think parents should realize that they cannot take the role of the teachers. They are not prepared for it. If parents don't allow the teachers to fill that space, the children will suffer from the emptiness the rest of their lives. So then, it requires togetherness.

When people come to the third institution, which is the Church, they can be fed with the word of God, which unifies the other two. Then they will know how to respect, to learn, and to be thankful for their accomplishments. They will learn how to thank God for all things. So, the Church has the last opportunity.

The Church can except only those who qualify themselves. Most people are so condemning when it comes to the Church. They never find the joy of salvation in the Church.

If you start with wrong ways, you can remove them through repentance only and start all over again. But the saddest part is when the child fails to keep time with the opportunities. You see, opportunities are always on time. They arrive at the right and proper time and knows when to arrive. If you are not able to meet that opportunity, to go to work and fulfill the responsibilities the opportunity has brought you, then that opportunity will leave and will not return. Opportunity comes only once. Another opportunity might come, but the same one will not. The child must be on time. That's why he or she has a beginning in the training, a beginning in education. It comes to be equal with the physical growth of that child, the development of the mind and the heart. and the function of the brain. These things must be on time. If a child wastes his or her time in the classroom at school, there's no way he or she can catch up. The child might fill in with some purpose, but they cannot catch what has been lost.

You cannot turn the bullet back when you have fired the gun. You just have to wait and see where it lands. You have to be ready so your target can be the right target. We must make sure these three institutions are together.

I think all parents should think about it when they are feeding their children's minds to be hostile towards other people. They are destroying what little they have done themselves.

Your teaching is completed only by the other two institutions. No one can make it through the world on home training alone. No one can make it through the world by education alone, what you gather at the school. No one can make it through the Church and get the fulfillment of what's available, the Spirit of God, unless you are in harmony with the things that make you what you are. It takes these things to make a lady or a man. It takes these things to build our principles and our intelligence—to qualify us to fit in, to qualify us to help build for others. It takes these God-fearing things. If you are in harmony with the other two, then the Church can make all things fit perfectly, and will give you the proper life in which to function. It will make you glad of every step or every effort you make. You'll feel like you have accomplished something. These three must work together. The parents, teachers, and ministers should know each other.

I don't believe you should wait until something drastic happens in your family for you to call the minister. You need to get advice from him before something happens.

You know, we have many people throughout the world who rely on their own conscious. They feel if they treat someone wrong, their conscious will tell them. They are right to a certain extent. But you don't want to live by your conscious, because your conscious doesn't speak until after you have done the wrong thing. Then your conscious starts nagging you. But, there's a Spirit, a comforter who speaks before you are guilty. He alerts you before you become guilty, because he speaks in time, moves in time, and directs in time. Therefore, you don't have to rely on your conscious. Your conscious proclaims your guilt. It interrupts your rest and your sleep because you are guilty. So then, the Church, through the Holy Spirit, is to certify your rank and good things in life and make them better, because it's the life of He who is set apart to be a part of that people.

Now, from the home you seek the school. From the school you seek the Church. From the homes and schools you seek jobs or positions. From the Church you seek life. So all of it has its rewards. All of these have their rewards; all of these have their promises. The home promises the schools it would render to that life the requirements it takes for you to use. We manifest what we bring into the world, and we raise them up just for you to take charge. You can't do what we have to do. It's our responsibility—our command from God—to bring them up and prepare them to move over in your department. That's what the home has promised boys and girls. We will discipline them. We will teach them to respect their elders. We will teach them to listen, to hear, and to seek for an understanding. Finding the means to be intelligent, we will see to it that they to become the next government representative, next neighbor, the next minister, or the next missionary. We will teach them so that when you get them, you will have all of the products you need to put this life together.

How many of you are failing? How many of you are living up to the promises of the school? The school officials say, "Come to us, and we'll get you ready. We'll prepare you to be a lawyer, a doctor in the medical world, or a musician, an actor, any other kind of professional throughout the world. We have help for whatever you want to be. We have it available for you. We're taking you because you came from the home. You give us the right materials with which to work, and we will produce a person with whom the church won't have problems. We promise to send you in all directions of the land—departments of companies, into businesses, into the air travels, industry, or into athletics. We will even give you a chance to have a sideline."

In the sideline, you have a chance to become a millionaire athlete. Let us understand, you will not go to school or to college to major to be an athlete. That's a sideline, but people have become millionaires because they were there. They had the proper conduct, and they were able to go there not just to work twelve or fifteen hours a day. Some have become millionaires as business men and women because of sidelines. This opportunity is what will happen when you follow up with and fulfill all of these activities; this is what life is all about. Those athletes did not go to school to be athletes only. They majored in something else. Some of them have gone back to school even after they had become professionals in different walks of life.

We need to teach them that when they move to the Church, there's another promise.

We promise—if you know how to listen, know how to conduct yourself, know how to understand one thing from the other, know how to recognize the department of life you are in—we will guarantee you life in Jesus Christ. This life is the product of the three united in harmony together. But if this life is not produced by working together, we all have a problem.

The home has a self-destruct capability by bringing up enemies. We train people how to be jailbirds. We train them to want something that does not belong to them. We never tell them you have enough; you don't need this. It's not a good time for this. We try to convince them they can have everything they want when they want it regardless of the cost. So, when they grow up, if they don't have something, they rob from the people who have it. If they don't have something, they crawl into somebody's window and steal it. If they don't have an automobile, they steal one for themselves. This behavior is what they have learned. They didn't learn it in those exact words, but they learned it. It's like being in a school and having grade levels. They moved up in grades according to what they were taught. They got everything they wanted.

When your child was wrong, you fought for them to make things right. When they did wrong, you hid things for them and told them you loved them. They felt they received extra love for doing wrong. Here are children doing wrong. They know they did wrong. You tell them you should whip them, but you love them. You say, "I would chastise you, but I love you." You love them for doing wrong? You love them for stealing from their neighbors? for stealing from the elderly? for stealing from friends? You love them for that? You love them because they blow the teacher out? You love them because they talk smart and act stupid to their teachers? You love them for that? If you love them for those things, your love for them is making them worse.

Our love has filled the jails and the prisons. They can't build them fast enough. Our love has people out there who will pass your house and shoot anybody. That's our love. That's our love out there, and it has made our community a dangerous place to live. Our love. And when our love stops working, we blame the government, we blame the schools, and we blame the church when we are guilty of it all. You did it at home. These children are what you sent from the home to the school and then to the church. And they can't fit into the church because they are condemned by everything you taught them. Every way you supported them, everything you committed to them was a condemnation.

How are you going to bring cleanliness out of unclean ingredients. You can't do it. Only God can do it. He's not going to do it, because you have violated every instruction. You violated the parents. You violated the teachers. You violated all of their instructions. Now you face the world. You are loose in the world, and your life is like an automobile with no brakes on it. It is just like a train running loose with no stopping power. It is just like a plane with no power in the air, and there's no place to go but down.

This kind of person is what we have turned loose out there by failing at home, in the school, and in the Church. A failure of the home, school, and Church is what we have.

We have everybody carrying guns. The guns are the killers, and the ones who are operating the guns, are fools.

Innocent people have suffered because of this kind of uncertainty, this change. We live among ourselves simply because we have failed with the three—the home, the school, and the Church. And all three can't get back together until the home, the parents, and the teacher communicate, talk, and reason together, because they are dealing with the same mind.

You can help the teachers by admitting your failures. If you tell them you have failed and what you have failed, the teachers will know how to deal with the problem. You know what you have failed to do. You know what you didn't do, and you know what you did and should not have done. Be honest. Save what you can from the child. Sit down and talk with the teachers. Tell them, "I failed at this, I failed at that." They will know more about how to deal with the situation. But after you have failed, you should not want to demand that the teacher follow up or blend in with your failure. That's wrong also. Two wrongs don't make a right. When you realize you're wrong, deal with it. Repent from it. Start over. Do the best thing. Try not to cover up. Try not to make it right. You can't make it right; right is right already. You have only one right. You have millions and millions of wrong things, but you have only one right. Just like the truth, you have only one truth. You have millions and millions of lies, but you have only one truth.

So then, if the problem is in the home (and most of it is in home), realize it. Don't say the teachers are not teaching them anything. The teachers are teaching, but the students are not hearing anything. They are not prepared to hear anything. They come to school angry at the teacher, because you told them at home that the teacher was not supposed to tell them what to do. The teacher is not supposed to hurt your feelings. The teacher is not supposed to send you out of the room. You have already told them, "I'm on your side." But you know what? When we were going to school, the parents were on the teacher's side. The parents supported the teacher because they wanted their child to have what the teacher had. The only way to get it was to go to school and to listen, respect, and obey.

So, when you fail at home, that's the beginning of your failure. When you come to school, you'll end up like anybody at school, except for the ones who are just like you. You come to Church, you're like anybody at the Church. Who are you? What do you intend to be? Come on parent...let's talk.

Let's look at ourselves. Let's look at what we're doing. Let's think about failures. Let's think about life. The physical life begins with us. Too many times it begins with the parents and ends with the parents. That child's life misses all the promises, all the plans, and all the preparations, Schools were built before that child was born. Teachers were prepared to go to work as soon as they were old enough.

Parents, you have destroyed it all. If the children don't make it through school, where are they going to make it? Where are they going? They don't know how they came to a junction which said "So not enter; it's dangerous." The only way they will enter is if they see someone else enter. Then, they get blown up, because they can't read the sign.

Isn't it sad. It's a failure that saddens all of us. We, as ministers, would like to do more, but most of the time, they are so twisted and destroyed when they get to us, it's almost impossible. It's sad. We preach to people and teach people, and we can't see any changes. The only thing we can see in their life is that they are getting older, and they are getting worse.

Can you imagine a man or a woman who has failed at everything? He flunked home, failed at the school, then come to the Church wanting to run it. He wants everyone to hear him, and he hasn't heard anyone. He has no credentials. He has no proof that he has been brought up by anyone decent. He wants everyone to listen to him. This behavior is what we find. It is what we run into. This situation is the one we meet, and it's hard to find the answer, even in books. As many books as are written, we face problems, and we just can't find the answers in books.

The cause of the separation of these three institutions belongs to the life that shapes a life which is responsible for the world in which we live. Until we realize that and make up our minds to go back to the old landmark and put our lives and responsibilities and all these things in their proper perspective, we are not going to get any better.

Government programs are not designed to make people anything. They are designed to help those who have made a mess of their lives. Bad teaching and bad discipline exist in our world today. Babies are having babies. And any time a young man becomes a father before he becomes a grown man, people suffer. Any time a young lady becomes a mother before she becomes a woman, people suffer. It is like a doctor going into a operating room when he has never been to medical school. You know what will come out of that room—dead people. He's going to kill them, because he knows nothing about medicine.

This description is the situation of our world. What should we do about it? Acknowledge that we have failed. Ask for repentance. Ask the Lord to guide us so that we might start over. And, by all means, we might save some. Get our sons and daughters to start rearing their children in the way that they should go, as the school should go, as the world should go, and as the government should go. If you want that, you have to raise it.

You know, some of our government people can come up with the strangest ideas. They think they can build a school and make a person what they want him to be. You can only remind them what they are and what they will never be, but schools don't make people. They bring out of people what they really are. Now, if they develop into proper material, the school helps to brings it out. Life comes from inside, not out. Nobody cuts open anybody in the classroom to put anything in them. School just brings out what's in them already. If they don't have it in them, and you make them go to school, they get worse. They get angry with their teachers; they get angry with everyone who does not agree with them. They just get angry with having to learn. Do you know how many students I have heard say, "I hate school," or, "I don't like going to school." They say that because school is hard for them. Everything is blocked out when it comes to action. They don't know how to act. They don't know how to show respect. They don't know how to trust. They don't know how to do anything. They don't have the capabilities within them or the potential to be taught. So it makes them angry. They get angry with themselves.

It's ridiculous how parents have told their children that they don't have to sit there and listen to what the teacher is saying. They'll just walk out of the classroom. They will walk out of the school. It's terrible because the unity has been broken between the institutions God established to make us what we should be.

Be aware parents, be aware ladies, the world can be only what you bring to it. Some dumb things that people are tied up in are things like abortion and shooting each other to death. These actions are not the way to deal with a situation. Go to the home. Tell the parents that they have failed.

You can't allow your daughters to ramble all night and expect them to be perfect in the morning. What do you think? You couldn't do it. How do you expect them to be alert when they are out all night? They are exposed to those who believe in staying out all night, and everyone knows they are not out there studying their Sunday School lesson. They are out there to get whatever they want and to do whatever they can do and get away with it. Parents who love their daughters don't lay down and go to sleep, and sleep soundly without knowing the whereabouts of their daughter. You don't know what's happening. You don't know where they are, or what might be happening to them. You sleep; you're resting well. No rules exist at home. If you don't have rules in your home, your home is the only place that doesn't have rules. Everywhere else there are rules. You can't drive your car and break the rules, you must have a driver's license. You must have insurance. You must have the sensibility to stop at stop signs. You have to obey speed limits. You have rules, rules, rules, and more rules.

THE THREE PERSONNEL
OF THE INSTITUTIONS

Parents, teachers, and the ministers—these three people should have strong fellowship and should always be in communication with each other, because their positions are the most important in the world. The world is shaped through our lives and how well we perform. We work, and we perform by leadership. We establish leadership. Leadership is not law. Leadership provides the proper leaders and followers. We lead in the most important ways, with all of our abilities and with all of our God-given strength. The physical world of the individual began by God himself saying, "Let us make man in our image, after our likeness; and let them have dominion over...every creeping thing that creepeth upon the earth." Now, we can understand God was not surprised by the down fall of man. He made it clear in His statement, as He saw the need for a chief creature of all His creation, that man around not continue in the image of Him. Many times we misunderstand or misquote the Scripture by saying we are made in the image of God. Only one man that was made in the image of God, and that man was Adam. Adam was made in the image of God, because the image of God is Holy, and Adam didn't hold out. He fell from the Holy stage. We are not made. We were the result of Adam's fall. So, God said," Let us make man in our image, after our likeness; and let them have dominion over the fish of the sea, and over the fowl of the air, and over the cattle, and over all the earth, and over every creeping thing that creepeth upon the earth." (Genesis 1:26). If you will notice, the text reads that He made one man, but He spoke, "Let us make man." So, the Lord knew this was the beginning of mankind, but man wouldn't continue to produce under this Holy situation. After the one man He made fell, the result of Adam's fall was that many men would be born. Therefore, many questions are asked concerning when God said, "Let us make man." Some would indicate there were men in other places, but the Bible doesn't give us that. The Bible says, "God said, Let us make man in our image, after our likeness, and let them..." (which means more than one) because many would come and many would serve and have dominion over all of the creatures. We are in indebted to God for getting our instruction from Him and living according to His instructions, because He made us the chief creatures of creation. He did not shut us out, but He had plans that we could later obtain this image of His. So, Adam was made, but we were born as a result of sin.

That's why it's important for us to experience the second birth. It's the only way we can take on the image of God. We are born sinners. We are born for destruction. We are born through destruction. As the scripture says, "Man that is born of a woman is of few days, and full of trouble." (Job 14:1).

We are born in trouble. We are born with trouble, but there's a plan that God works through the physical stage of man. And he man might have a better attitude, and even be shaped through the physical shape of life, if he were able to understand through leadership and to find existing institutions, that might restore him back to the holiness of God. This is being restored by being born.

The first work and responsibility is the home and the family. The family is the entity which produces life in the beginning of the physical stage.

I think we need to study more about the importance of the contributions we make to the world through our lives and through families. Without children being born, there can be no generations, no world for us, and no one to come. The parents must understand the importance and the sacredness of their responsibility in the home, because the community, the schools, the government, and the entire world can be only what the home and the parents produce. I think we should think about the beginning, and instead of fighting each other and destroying each other, we should seek common sense. And common sense is the development and the making of the child. Children are born shaped in iniquity and full of troubles, meaning they don't need additional troubles. They are born ignorant into this world they have never seen before. They are born into a world where they have to live. They have to fill a position in this world, which means that first the children must be developed, and they are developed by the human experience that is planned by God Himself. But all have not followed the Lord's instructions.

The child is developed from his mother. He is developed from the mind, body, and soul. All the attitudes and experiences this woman goes through for nine months is the crucial time of anyone's life.

You are being developed. You are being developed, not from dust, not from nothing, but from the motherhood—from, the mother who brings you into the world. The mother should begin building the personality, the attitude, and the direction that she would have the child go, as well as the kind of attitude that she would prefer her child to have by demonstrating it herself in this short period of time.

I think you should refrain from all excitement, from things that upset you, from things that frighten you, and from things that cause you to be abused. I think we should remember back to the time when pregnant women weren't allowed to look at the face of a dead person or to be around any bloody or grieving people. We should keep peace of mind and not to be aggravated by what others are doing or what others are saying.

When we conduct ourselves in the right manner, we have beautiful branches developing from us. The branch that springs from the tree has the same nature as the tree. It brings the same type of fruit. You must remember the things you eat and drink, the kind of medication you use, and the kind of language you speak.

We have qualified people to tell us what we should and should not drink, and what we should do for the betterment of this child who is being developed from our minds, our bodies, and the way we conduct ourselves. So, when the child comes into the world, he or she comes in the meekness and into a helpless situation.

Children bring nothing with them but hopelessness. Someone fulfills their needs, and there is provision made for them when they arrive.

We need to assist the mother or parents of the home with the ingredients of a good life that can only be produced by the home. We can be sure that if children receive this proper arrival and exposure to the preparations that are made for them, they it can catch on in their proper place.

There is education in spiritual life where we have no problem catching on to its rightful place. But these children must be disciplined in the mind—not with some club, not by being abused or misused, but by hoping that they develop with the proper attitude. They have been developed by the proper resources to organize their minds and their conditions and to prepare themselves for the opportunities that are planned for them as they enter a world they know nothing about. They are able to accept those who greet their little beautiful babies, those who are willing to share, and those who wait to contribute to them.

I think that before we fail to destroy the world, let us remember that it is not ours. We found this world. We found the government. We found the community functioning and doing well. We should remember these things as we grow up and as we move from one stage of life to another.

Young people, you should be made aware that you are made up of contributions only. Everything about you was given to you. Your mother gives you birth, along with the anticipation of your father. Your mother bought the pains of your arrival. If everyone who had given to this life and its existence were to call and request their gift back, there wouldn't be even a shatter left. If the mother said, "Give me back my pain," and the father said, "Give me back my sweat and my support in the part that I played in the development; if they who taught you how to walk, who taught you how to stand, who taught you how to talk, would say, "Give it back;" if the teacher said "Give me back the knowledge that I have shared with you;" if the doctor said "Give me back my medical experience;" if everyone were to just take away, we would become nothing, because there would be nothing left.

So, we don't come into this world to tear it up, because it's not ours. We came in to be thankful for whatever has made us what we are. It's not the purpose of parents to make us what we are. It's not the purpose of parents to make us murderers and thieves and all of the other people that produce this grief of the human family. You didn't realize what position the child would be in when he or she came into this beautiful world. I think that you should strive to have something to rejoice about. When you can see the little child, you can imagine where he or she will perform. The child has become such a great asset to the human family.

When you look at your child becoming a doctor, a lawyer, or another professional or government official who contributes so much to making the world better, you should be grateful, and you should turn to the Lord and give Him praise for the rest of your life. We seem to want to give the credit to some other source, and there are many ways, now, that we can give precious things. But remember this, only God can give you life. Only God can take it away. So the parents have a major role. The parents have been well supported in their child's downfall.

I think there are other people who have overstepped their bounds and have risen up against the things about life that God has said are very good. As God was creating, and as He made us and the things around us, He would pause many times and say, "It's good, or it is very good." Later on, the men who came and who were born in sin shaped iniquity and were moved not by the inspiration of God but by the studies of a materialistic world. He found God's plans and God's way unfit for the people of the places that He had made.

We have a problem with several situations that have an effect upon us, one way or the other. One great problem that we have is the mother and the baby.

God has always, in every female, regardless of what it is, given the mother the means and the know-how beginning the feeding of her young ones. Each creature that he made, which required milk, He gave the mother milk. He gave the mother formula so that she can be the right pattern, the right image, and the right person for this child. He did not give her someone else's milk; He gave her milk for her child, for her little baby.

The medical world says the milk is unhealthy; the milk is no good. Now that's a problem. Cow's milk is good for cows; goat's milk is good for goats, and every other creature that begins the nursing of the body through milk, the milk is still working. But the human being's mother's milk had to be substituted with cow's milk and goat's milk. I wonder if this substitution of milk had a strong bearing on the development of the child. The cow's milk, the goat's milk, the human being—do they have any reaction to goats and cattle? Are their minds affected? Why is it the entire world (and generations) have lost their God-like way of feeding their own children?

That's a problem, and I think someone needs to address these questions and work on these problems. It does make a difference. I'm not a medical person, but I would like for someone to tell me, because I'm concerned about it. I'm sure there are others who are concerned about it too.

Look at our little boys and girls doing unusual things. It's amusing to us; we laugh about it. We give them credit for being so smart so small. But we fail to think about the fact that a child has no business being an adult as soon as he or she is born. How are you going to be an adult without growth? How can you become an adult before you become a teenager? How can you be an adult before you know anything about the responsibilities of life, the world you live in, the things you see, or the things before you?

If you treat a child like an adult long enough, he will feel like an adult. Life is developed in the growth to maturity, and if you do away with the mature ideas, they will be ignorant in the way of understanding what it's all about. You cannot be a man until you grow to be a man so you can accept a man's responsibilities. We find the truth about it because when any boy becomes a father before he becomes a man, people suffer. Any time a young lady becomes a mother before she becomes a woman, people suffer. The world is affected, and your community is affected by this kind of carrying on. The person is affected the rest of his or her life and doesn't know what position he or she holds.

You make a great jump. How can a doctor be a doctor without going to medical school? How can a doctor go from elementary school to the operating room? That can't happen.

To accomplish the things we have in life, we're going to have to go through the times and we're going to have to go through the plans that are laid out for developing these kinds of men and women. We're traveling too fast. We want everything to happen overnight. We can't wait. We want to live twelve months in one day. It just won't work. We'll drive seventy-five miles an hour from the country store to our house, which is only two or three miles. And we will pass someone to cut in front of him to quickly make the turn that will cause a wreck. We are in too big of a hurry to do nothing.

The problem still remains, what happened with the milk? What becomes of the milk—the mysterious way that God can give to a human being or anything else? Only God can let a cow go out and eat green grass and produce white milk. Only God can gives others, especially women, the kind of food they eat and let it become the God-given food for their babies. Well, if it is no good or if it is stopped or suspended by the doctors, you can't get rid of all of it because it is God's work. So what happened to it? Did it dry up? Did you take the mother-like abilities? Did it completely cut loose from your health? I doubt that. If the milk is not used, what becomes of it?

I remember when I was brought up, and many of you, too. When we were brought up and were nursed by our mothers, we didn't hear about breast cancer and all of the other cancers that are appearing in the woman's body. Where did this come from? I'm not saying it is, but I wonder, does the milk problem have anything to do with this? I don't think you can move God's way out of the way, clean it up, and never see an effect one way or the other. Any time you rise up against God, it's an unequal match. If you change God's plan, you have a problem you can't wash away. Whenever you try to correct God, you come out on the wrong side. Nobody can outmatch God; nobody can make what God has made for something else and expect it to be something better than what God had made.

So what happens? Is it for the best, or is it for the worse? I think this milk question has a bearing upon those who are brought up. They have to be little related to the cow or to the goat, because they were developed with the ingredients of the cow's nature. Now the cow's milk is good for us. (That's what my doctor says.) It's good for us to drink it, but it is not good for the babies. It's no good for the mother to use to nurse the child. It's a problem. I think it is important to explain and to look into it to find out if the best choice has been made. That's a great portion of our problems in life, in our health and in our relationships. It opens the doors for diseases that are incurable and are causing our physical lives to be destroyed.

The home should be given more respect. When you interfere with the life, you are drawing a mountain between you and your creator that you cannot get around. God will not have anyone tampering with his handiwork. God is still God. He said "I am the Lord thy God, and I change not." So you can't change God, and he is so perfect that there is no way for Him to change. God cannot change. Change to what? He's so much in control. To what would He change? There's nothing for Him to change to. Like us, when we're wrong, we try to get right. If we don't understand certain things in life, we study and try and learn. But God knows everything. He doesn't have to change. He doesn't make a mistake. He's truth. That's why one word mastered truth all by itself. One word.

Our main problem in the home, in the physical stage of life, is that we have left God out of it. We're trying to do it ourselves. But it's impossible, because God, and only God can control life. Only God can change life from one stage to another. To bring up children in an ungodly manner is a great mistake. That's a defect not only to your children, but throughout their lives. This is the responsibility of the family at home to teach our children the rules of the home; the community, the state, and the world.

Our homes and our schools depend upon the job we do at home and with our families.

Let us think about when a child is born. We are talking about the most important number one institution of the three. Look at us when a human child is born. What do we see when we look on the face of that child? The mother, the parents, the neighbors look on that child only to see how he looks, who he favors, the nationality (light or dark), or some other useless idea that really doesn't touch the important purpose of that child's being born into this world. This is what we look for, and many times, when we conclude and find the answer to what we see, we really don't see that for which we are looking. When you're looking into this baby's laughing face, you really don't know at what kind of person you are really looking. You don't know what that baby will become—a doctor, a lawyer, a governor, the president, a professional of some kind, a father, a minister, a missionary, etc. But that could be the very face into which you're looking. That's what you should look for, because when you look at that child's face, you're looking at your next family person. Also, you are looking at your next home, your next school, your next church, your next community, your next state person, and your next country person, and if you can see this, you should realize what your responsibilities are.

These responsibilities are to start seeking and preparing the child for something other than the desire to compete—to be better than other children—to have things other children don't have, to be the child to whom other children have to look up, or to be the child in the community who is worshipped. At Christmas, this child gets a truck load of gifts, and the other children get nothing. This is what we set out to do, not to look across or in front or on the left or right at the less fortunate one, but we look down on the one who doesn't have anything. This is what we place a value on or support. We support that with all the means we have. We want a child to go to school to complete our selfish desires in the child's life not realizing that one child cannot be a community. One child's well being cannot answer for all the other suffering children. One rich child cannot have any mercy or peace of mind for the poor, but through each other, all together, we can have the good things of the world. All could have the good pleasure or could appreciate the sunshine and the rain. But if they are not looked upon as the community and looked upon in hope for a better community, then we get off on the wrong foot. We should be able to hope that our children can learn about themselves and learn about others, and when they see that they are human beings like others, then they will understand and will be willing to share their compassion, their love, and their respect for others. If this understanding doesn't happen to them, they cannot be the next community.

I think we all should feel some guilt over the community and the world in which we live. We have failed to produce. We have failed to bring forth the kind of community to represent people of common sense, people of unity, people of respect, and people who could live in a world where we are all trapped together.

It's sad that the only way we can show ourselves neighborly to each other is when tragedy storms, or high water occur. We can't live in a community together, but we can stay as long as it takes in a shelter together. We go to the shelter together to protect our lives, because we are in danger. We don't look at color. We don't look at the pride we had before. We don't look for racism. We look for a way to survive. Everyone wants to survive. If we can unite in the spirit of survival when our lives are in danger, and not have common sense to respect each other when things are well, then we don't deserve the things that the Lord has given to all of us. We really don't deserve them. The children can bring forth only that in which we help them to be mature. The child brought up in hate will overlook his human responsibility. It's going to be a problem. It's going to be a problem the rest of his life and the rest of your life. It brings about greed and madness. How can we be proud of ourselves when these are our children. Dopeheads. These are our children murdering each other. These are our children climbing in our neighbors' homes. These are our children; they are the fruit of our harvest. Whenever our harvest came, and we gathered what we had that day, we should have all gone to our knees and stayed there until the Lord forgave us and gave us a chance to do better, because we have done a poor job.

The Lord put us to a test, because He gave us a beautiful world in which to live and filled it with blessings. We're blessed more now than ever in history, and we're more ungrateful. When we think of how we are surrounded with blessings, then we are concerned about the things we don't have, and we are less thankful for what we do have. I've never understood how people who live in the strongest, most prosperous, and most beautiful country on the land can go out downcast on every hand. The government is no good. The school is no good Nothing is any good. Many of our young people are finding things are no good, because they are getting it from the adults. There are a lot of questions, and the questions that the children ask is if the government or the politicians are no good, and if they have done everything wrong, how did we produce all of what our eyes can see, our conveniences, and the world in which we live? Materially, how did these things come about? If the government is no good, who built this government with its democracy? If the people in Washington are no good and haven't done anything, and if they are who you say they are, who built the White House? Who arranged all of this? It has become their enemy. We have taken them for our enemy instead of appreciating their knowledge, their insights and their accomplishments with the help of God.

The young people can't hear anything good. Openly, the president is no good, the government is no good, the representatives are no good. There is something wrong with everybody except the man running for office. Now, common sense will tell you, how can the man running for office have more qualifications and proof of anything better than the man who is in the office? Or how can he who has never been to Washington do more than the people who have been to Washington? If he could get there, what would he do in the White House? What more can he do than what has been done already. We forget as we experience the blessings that come with the times. We find out that we don't need someone to stay in the office for more than a short time. The question is, how can anyone conduct business in a country such as America by spending his life learning how? Every time an individual gets there and learns how, we get rid of him and want someone else to come and do it, and he doesn't know how.

How long do you think the country is going to last? You are blessed to have experience. You are blessed to have people who know what to do and who are not learning while somebody else is doing a good job. Instead of destroying the good that they are doing, let it be a lesson. Let it be an objective in your mind and prepare yourself to think that you might carry on equally. You may have an opportunity to do a little better, but that depends upon the blessings from God.

It's sickening for a man or for a group of men anywhere—in the government, or at home, or anywhere—to clearly promise you what you are going to be doing in five to ten years from today when you don't even know if you are going to be living that long. You don't know what the conditions may be. God sends the rain. God sends progress. God makes the addition, not man. Trust in the Lord, and prepare to receive and appreciate whatever the Lord gives to you.

Why destroy each other for pride and to be in the spotlight? The light doesn't shine forever, Heroism is a short life. Heroes don't live forever; they don't last long. If you are a hero in boxing, one punch will knock you out of being a hero and put you in the back of the comic books. When you become famous you have reached the peak. If you are building fame, you have something to look forward to, but when you become famous, you're at the peak. There's no place to go but down; nowhere to go but in the record book. You've had it! Why can't we appreciate knowledge and appreciate a lot of the experiences which were brought together for the betterment of people, the community, the great fellowship towards each other?

Why is it so easy for us to turn away and go after people who have no evidence to back up their promises? A man comes in and tells me that he is going to do something about this *no good government*, because this government is no good. I've read him already. What can you do about it? You don't know anything about it. Why should I throw away something I have for something I know nothing about. Common sense keeps us in a strong attitude and keeps us in the condition to think before we speak and to evaluate, day by day, our strength and our ability to do before we try to pull down others. You cannot become great by pulling down someone else. If you overcome anything, you have to come by someone. Someone has to help you to become anything in life. You can't become, you can't reach the peak, you can't reach the top of the mountain by yourself. Somebody has to help you along the way. So, then, negativism has destroyed possessiveness, and we are doing it everyday. Positive thinking comes up too late. Negative is our motto.

It makes you sick when professional people who know better use these things in order to warp people's minds. They address these kinds of statements and attitudes, and they throw it out to confuse people's minds. They react to what you are saying or what you are trying to do.

We are great supporters of nothing. We are great supporters in downcasting; we are slow to build up. These people are the kind of people we have brought forth. These people are the kind of fruit that came from our labor. So, then, as children are born let us look for what we want in their faces. When we look into their faces let's thank God and ask Him, "Is this where a better community starts? Is this the kind of person from whom we are suffering? Is this one of them, is this two of them?"

How many small, and born, children are we beholding? We seek, regardless to who they are, to what community they belong, or what color they are. Let's look for a neighborhood. Let's look for a government. Let's look for a school. Let's look for all it takes to build a community and the world I which we live.

If we look for these attributes, then our minds will focus on rendering a share to the cause. Out of these lives will come a better community than what we have brought forth. There are things in life that we take for granted and turn our backs on. We miss the mark, and we suffer the consequences later. I think that we should stop look at ourselves, and look around us, and stop pointing at the other guys We should look at ourselves and say, "We have failed. We must do something about it. There are some things that must be done together." One person, one race, one color, or one nationality cannot build the kind of world that God would have it to be. It takes every person to contribute to the cause, because everyone who comes into this world faces the same responsibilities. You either enjoy what you have invested in the community in which you live, or you suffer the consequences of your failure. You either bring up the child where he or she can bring joy and prosperity and has the fear of the appearance of God in his or her life, or you suffer the consequences, because you fail through them.

I like to remind us that it is not so much the young people who are failing today. They are failing. The failures are falling, but they are not failing alone. They are failing with us. We fail to plant in them the right kind of seed to bring forth the right kind of fruit, the right behavior, the right kind of love, the right attitude towards each other, the right kind of compassion, and the right kind of the ability to be thankful and faithful over a small amount so it can grow into a large amount.

There are some situations concerning our young people for which it is to late to do anything about. That's why the alternative now is to try to build more prisons and jails. We are trying hard to slow down the speed of disaster. There are some things we could bring down to a minimum, slow the pace, but there are some things that we cannot change, because if a person is mature in destruction, that's one area you can't clean up. A living soul—a life—only God can sanctify. God does not let us by with wrongdoing without paying the price. So, we have to suffer through, but we could make a better life for those coming behind us. We have to put our shoulders to the grinding stone and go to those who are being born into the world now.

It's a difficult problem that the parents can't do alone; it's going to take grandparents to do it. Your problem now is that you have children having children, and it's impossible for the children to know about the importance of the steps in time to take with a child.

You really can't be the kind of mother that you should be if you haven't been a woman first. When you become a mother first, there is too much space. There is too much vacancy in your life, and there is too much knowledge missing. There is too much missing information in your life to face the problems and responsibilities of life.

We have to try and help them to blunder through life and, at the same time, do a better job with those who have a chance, which are those who are being born and those who are to be born in our community. Let us turn and give our best shot, because it would be a shame for us to live in a world of prosperity and plenty and allow a worse situation to come after us with what we have done. I think we should learn from our mistakes. We should turn and contribute much, because we have failed. We have a chance to overcome. We are not talking about machinery. We are not talking about things, We are talking about human lives. We are talking about people. We are talking about the creature that God exalted above all other creatures— the only upright creature that the Lord chose to have dominion over the other creatures. But ignorance can destroy. It's next to sin. Sin will keep you from getting a start, but ignorance will destroy you anytime in life, anytime of day.

So, we have to learn. We have to seek what's right. We have to learn what's right and ask God for the courage to do it. It must be done in time. It is no use to let children grow up and have their way in everything. When they grow up to become a teenagers, we try to shape them as we should have in their early years.

Hopefully you will get this message so that you will understand that to have a community, it must be born It must be reared in the lives of human beings. You don't wait until harvest time to plant. You don't plant on top of the ground. You plant under the ground and harvest on top of the ground, if you know what I mean. You have to plant before you can harvest, and you cannot plant and harvest at the same time. The plant as to be a seed before it becomes a bulb. You have to be a flower before you become fruit. This is human life. It is our responsibility to see what is missing in our lives and in our community and our reasons for it. We can do something about it. We have made the job very difficult, but, by all means, we can save some. This important department of life, this institution, must totally perform its responsibility in order to get lives ready to move to the next one. If life is not given its full opportunity in the home, it will have a difficult time adjusting to the next one. What I'm saying is if you haven't been exposed to responsibilities or prepared at home, it's very difficult for you to step into the school and fully benefit there. Your school experience will depend upon what happens at home. We have not only these things that we might experience—better living and better communities—but we are also held responsible for our failures.

Look what happens when we fail. Many people die unnecessarily. Many people's lives are just snuffed away for no reason at all. Drive-by shootings occur in the house. Children are being killed without a chance to know anything about the world in which they were born. The failure at home took away a lot of prosperity in the home, and we had to answer to the destruction that came out of our failure. It's our failure that causes so many prisons to be built and so many lives to be lost. It's our failure that causes so many diseases to come upon us. These things occur simply because of our failure to turn to God. Even we can turn to God and ask Him to forgive us with the intentions that we want to do better. God will forgive, but we are going to pay the price. People will tell you, if God forgives you, He cleans the slate. God will forgive you, but His word says you are going to pay, and if God says you are going to pay, you are going to pay. So, if sin comes to our house, it's going to be with us the rest of our lives. But it's so good when we can see our mistakes. Even if we spend our lives in sweat and heartache, we know when we finish our cause, and whatever punishment may occur when our life is finished, we have a life to which we can look forward—not here, but in eternity, which is the best.

We have to stop where we are and count the cost. We have to be honest and look at the situation in our homes, our shortcomings at home. There are too many replacements. Judges cannot know what's better for the children than the mother or father; it's impossible. It's impossible for the school board to discipline the children when they don't know the problems the children have at home. Only the teacher knows—the teacher who has control over the classroom. The school board does not have control over the classroom. Its members are someplace else doing other things, and the teachers are there, fearing for their lives because they have a bunch of loose-minded kids with whom they are dealing.

The law is saying let them have their way and at the same time, learn. It's as if they were trying to wear two left shoes at the same time. That can't work. There is going to have to be a lot of changes made. I think even the government and the judges realize it's not working. It's not working. It brings a certain amount of pain and resentment for the children to wake up and realize that foster parents are not their parents. Sometimes conditions bring that action—to adjust to every little blunder or every little move that you think gives you a reason to take the children from the parents and take them somewhere else.

My God, you have most of us. We don't beat them up. We feed them. We give them clothes to wear. But we don't feed anything to the mind. We fill their stomachs. We stop their crying. We take them to the doctor and get their medication, but we don't give them the issues of life, the general principles. Man should not live by bread alone. We give them a bed, but we rob them of the life. Souls cannot eat bread. Souls can survive only by the Word of God. When we rob them, we rob them of their minds—their spiritual minds and their physical minds. It doesn't matter about them having clothes or fine homes in which to live. It's not so much the house in which they live, it's what is supposed to live in them. We can't train people by rubbing something on them or by showing them movies or films to see how other people are doing.

They don't have the kind of common sense that loves the seed planted in the mind even to absorb what the eyes see. You see a lot of things you can't figure out. A lot of other people can perform better than you, but that doesn't make you know how to do it. You might not ever be able to do whatever you see other people do. If you don't have it in you, it can't work. Out of the heart comes the issues of life. Life comes from the inside. Life is not in a jar of ointment or a bottle of liquid that you pour on someone. Life makes up life, and you have to start in time. You have to start when children are children, not when they are grown. You can't rub it on them; it has to grown in them.

The language of our children is disgusting. As I said before, many of them can spell "yes sir," "yes ma'am," and "thank you," but they won't say it. They don't say it; it's not important to them. They have no way to practice these words; they have been blotted out. Children practice their discipline. They practice their language at home on their parents. The way in which they speak to their parents is the way they are going to speak to everyone else. If it's not "sir" to their father, it's not going to be "sir" to anyone else. They are not machines; they are human beings, and it would be a formality to disrespect your father and be kind and friendly to other men or to disrespect your mother and talk to her as if she were a person from out of the clouds and be humble and kind to others. It doesn't work that way.

THE FIRST INSTITUTION: THE HOME

Let's take a good look at our home—our home and our family in the home. What can we do about the crimes and the danger in our homes? A better question is what are we doing about it? Nothing. That's why they are there. What can we do about it? Stop it. Nobody can stop it but us. How can we stop it? We can come together as a family as citizens, and as neighbors. I wonder if you know anything about that. Come together. If you do that, you'll stop it. A thief knows when you say you don't want to be involved. He knows that your uninvolvement is his hiding place. Many times someone sees someone else doing things. We see it and do nothing, and we blame others for not getting involved. This behavior is the fruit of our doing nothing.

We blame the policeman. The policeman can't be everywhere or have his eyes everywhere at the same time. We would have to have as many policemen as there are fowls in the air. You don't need policemen to sleep on your porch. You need policemen when you see these crimes begin to form. But you don't want to be involved. I have news for you. Let me tell you a secret. You are involved. When a thief finishes the other house, your house is next. When someone is breaking into the other house, someone else is creeping around your house. Therefore, we are involved. So why don't we protect each other? Why don't you let what you see be used by those who are prepared to take charge? How can the policeman solve the problem when we saw the problem and he didn't? He has to guess. He has to investigate. He has to find out who did what and when we witnessed it. We witnessed it, and we just don't want to be involved.

When we turn from what the Lord has made us we can become blind over simple things. Some things that are so simple they seem as if there is a mountain before us, but we can't see it.

Let us think about what happens, what comes from our uninvolvement. Lot's of things happen. Vandalism, kidnapping, and dope penetrate through our community. All of these things come because of our uninvolvement. Don't you know that the smartest thing people's neighbors can do in the community is be supporters of the police officers. If we support them they will protect us. We see the crime; let them solve the problems. Come out and say," Yes this is the one," or call the policemen and let them come to save lives and save us from destroying our own community. We are being destroyed. Our children are being kidnapped. Our homes are being vandalized, and we say we don't want to be involved. How involved can you be? It's your children. It's your property. It's your home, and I think that the worst thing that is involved in the whole situation is your mind. Your mind is not telling you to do anything. Lives are being lost, because you aren't doing anything, and the greatest support that you can give to any criminal is to do nothing. What comes out of nothing? Nothing! It's hard to understand why a lot of people invest too much in nothing, and you should ask the question," What is nothing?" What is nothing? Can you describe nothing? You can't see it. You can't feel it. You can't taste it. You can't use it. It's just nothing.

We think of the things that are happening, and somebody is hurt, and we have witnessed it. We have witnessed the movement, and sometimes we have seen the victim. Sometimes we have seen all that are involved, and we did nothing. How do we feel after the child is missing? How do we feel after the home is destroyed? How do we feel about what has been accomplished after we did nothing? So you want to clean up the community? You want to get the thieves? You want to get the killer? You want to get the dope dealers out of your community? You didn't get involved, not as policemen, not trying to become heroes, but by just picking up the telephone, just walking out and being a witness that will last always. That will drive this type of filth out of your community. Then you can sleep well at night. You can be assured that our children can play together and that they will learn a lesson about how to protect each other. Let us not continue to teach our children not to become involved, but teach them to tell the truth. Teach them to tell what they saw, tell what they know, tell those who are available to do something about whatever is going on. The policemen can be no better than what we are. They cannot perform any better than we support and help them when they did not see the crime. How do you expect the policemen to solve it when we are the ones who know about it? Give it to them. Give it to them before it happens, and sometimes you can prevent it from happening.

Think about your family. Think about other families. Think about your community. You can only produce a community made up of what it depends upon and for what it stands for. When we help the community become a group of thieves, those who are able to buy a home somewhere else will move out to a more quiet place where they can rear their children the way they should be reared. If you practice the same thing in your new community, it won't take long for it to become the same kind of community you left. You can't outrun your problems. Your problems can outtravel you. You have to get rid of them.

Your condition is sin. Wrongness is sin, and sin is always there. You can't run from sin, but you cannot yield to it. You see, you don't make sin, you accept sin. It doesn't matter what crime you may commit, if it's sin many others have committed that crime long before you. So, there is no such thing as your committing the first sin, because too many generations have come and gone, and they were all exposed to the same sin.

There was sin before Jesus. It was sin that came from the first man. There was sin before the flood, it was sin after the flood. Jesus came and died for our sins, but sin is still around. We still support sin rather than grace. Sin will tell us not to get involved. Compassion will tell us to be honest and to do unto others what we will have them to do unto us. If this doesn't happen, you can see others' children getting kidnapped, and the only thing that you can give them is some tears and flimsy talk about being sorry and what somebody else ought to do. Nobody else saw this crime. You saw it. And when you saw it, you should have become a responsible citizen and called for help and reported it to the authorities so they could do the job they are prepared to do.

How can we clean our community? We can go back to where we failed and realize that we cannot raise our children alone. We need every parent to help us to be good parents. We need every parent to watch over and protect the integrity of our children. You can't see your children at all times. You are pleased at what you see, because they are smart enough to be real good children as long as you are looking. You don't know their capability to commit the crimes that are happening throughout the country. Every time some man or some person picks up a gun and loses his mind and starts shooting and killing innocent people, somebody comes out and says, "I don't understand. He was a good person." And the parents come and say he never did anything wrong, he has been a good person, and he didn't bother anybody. Did your neighbors tell you that? Who told you he was good while you were looking. He was performing while you were looking. What do your neighbors have to say? Can they attest that this person has been a real good citizen and say it's a mystery how he can just change over night? Come on, let's get together. Come on, let's do our duty as a citizen. Let us unite ourselves with all people who play a major role in making our community safer and protecting our homes the lives of our children, and our lives. When we fail to carry out our duties, we let down the principles of our community.

The police officers need us, and we certainly need them. Put the witnesses and police officers together, and support each other. The work is there. We have a job to do. We're safe and our children are well. The policemen are glad, because they were able to their job—what they are suppose to do.

You want to know why they are handicapped, why they can't do any better. Because, they cannot do the impossible. They have to spend too much time on one crime. The jails are overcrowded. They have to let criminals go free, because they have no place to put them.

Yes, the authority have to spend too much time on one crime. They're spending the time trying to track down individuals, trying to put pieces together, trying to question the whole community concerning one particular person. You know, when you think about it, how does a community of people look? How do they feel when something happens in their community and the policemen come and have to question everyone in the community concerning that one crime? The investigators come looking for evidence—clues on that one crime. Investigators spend weeks, or months, years investigating one person. Others are locked up waiting until they get through. The policemen are trying to find out information you already know. The only thing you have to do is step forward, tell them what you saw, and tell them who it was.

Let's underline this point; tell them what you saw. If it was your son crawling into your neighbor's window, tell the policeman. That will help that man. Yes, that will help him. He would have to come only once. But when you protect the criminal and let him get away with this crime, that prepares him. He thinks this is the best way of life—making a living doing nothing. So, if you can't stop him from crawling into your neighbor's window, report him to the authorities. They can help change his mind and change his attitude.

We see the results of our failure. The courtrooms are overflowing. The jails are all filled. The prisons are filled. The criminals are being let out early, and they go back to doing the same thing they were doing just because you refuse to become involved. Take my word for it. You are involved. You are the victim. Everyone who sees, and does nothing about it, is the next victim. You see little boys and girls walking down the street. Cars stop and pick them up, kidnap them, and you say nothing about it. You are involved because that same crowd may have its eyes on your little child.

Get involved We can make a difference at home. The home controls the world. The home is a part of the earth. Many people don't know that their livelihood comes from the earth. You abuse the earth. You think the food you have just fell from the sky. No, no, it comes from the earth, and we should think about it. Our home, the world, the land, the community, and the government all depend upon what's going on at home. Crime is out of hand simply because our neighborhoods are not involved. You are involved. The problem begins with you.

We have produced bad apples, and since we realized it and came out of our homes, someone wants to help us, wants to help us solve these problems and put things on the safe side. We can, at last, help them to correct some of our wrongs.

When you don't report a crime, you are doing the wrong thing because you helped to create the crime. You helped to cause the crime not by advising or teaching someone how to do it, but by doing nothing, by not doing the things in the proper time, and by not having support or help from someone else.

You have fired the neighbor, and you have moved under your own little vine. You say you don't need someone to tell you about your child. When someone tries to tell you that your child is getting loose, he or she becomes your enemy, because your precious child can do no wrong. You can't say that. In spite of all your efforts, that child has a mind of his own. The child has an opportunity to do right or wrong. You don't see the child at all times. When the child heads in that direction, you might not know about it, because you don't allow your neighbors to tell you anything about your child.

That's why this country is what it is today, because neighbors live and protect each other. They prevent crime. They prevent children from going astray, because they report to each other the children's movements, even the small things that the children were doing. It is the small things that create large things. Wrong grows. It never stays the same. If the children get away with picking up packs of chewing gum, and if they're not stopped, the next time they will pick up something bigger. This thievery will get larger each time they commit a crime. Then, before you know it, they have gotten themselves into the system. They have found a way of getting something for nothing. Some of them get a kick out of doing this. They can be smart and be slick, and they feel as if they have out-smarted everyone else. There are many reasons why they began playing games or doing wrong. It becomes useful to them, and it becomes a part of life.

There's a need for each other's protection. Yes, the neighbor who lives in the back of your house, sees the back of your house more than you do. The neighbor who lives on either side of you, sees that side of your house much more than you do. The part of the house that you see most is the front part, because you go in and out that way. So, for a neighbor to be nice and look out for you, pick up the phone and say look out, be careful. They are afraid, because you are charging them with interference.

That just builds up. We have gotten to the place now where good men—and good family men and Christian men—can hardly smile and say good morning to a lady. They may be charged with harassment. We can come up with some of the most ridiculous things— anything to bring a wedge between the human's well-being and the problems he gains. Of course, poor people, poor men, won't have to worry about that, because women usually make these reports about men who have money so that they can get an easy way out. There is always something to gain, but it destroys the human's intelligence. I realize most people go too far in everything, so I realize that there are men who smile at a lady and say good morning, and the lady wants him. But that's a small minority. Most men appreciate the kindness, because they try, to the best of their ability, to express the same. Certainly they can't express sunshine as well as the ladies do. Ladies are made for that kind of reaction, but in their hearts they appreciate the respect and kindness.

We are going to make laws that you can compliment someone by saying, "You look well; you dress well," but you better watch how you say it, because you might end up with a harassment charge.

Little foolish and petty things destroy and cause more misery that comes into our lives instead of happiness. We always have something to make us miserable even in our own homes. Let us wake up and realize that our failure has contaminated our community. It has given the thieves a hiding place. It has invited our enemy to come in and destroy our community. Let us all in the household be strong men. Jesus said one day, "You cannot default what's in the house until you bind the strong man of the house." Let's be strong and flexible, and let us remember that we are not the only men who exist.

Sometimes we are disgusting to the people in our community. We look for certain people in our community. Many people have moved out of our community, because they don't like who has moved in. If we are together, then we shouldn't have to do ugly things to drive someone out of our community. If they are not able to join in with our principles and our action and protection, they are not going to continue living there. They are going to move. If they are willing to join in our protection, our police help, and our effort to keep our community safe, to keep the thieves and criminals out of it, so be it. We need those kind of people in our community.

But we prefer to have criminals in our community if they are the right color. That's nonsense! You allow and prepare. You close eyes so the robber or the murderer can penetrate your neighborhood. You don't want citizens that can make your community better. You prefer the people who destroy you over those who will help you build up a community just because of the color of their skin. That's a hot one. You don't have to be smart to see that there are holes all through it. There is nothing you can get out of that to make living better. There is nothing you can gain out of it but hate, weakness, and no respect for human beings.

Let's think about this. Every person who is a kidnapper, or a thief, is not a black person. Every person who robs is not a black person. It is not the color that is doing the job. It is not the outside of the person that is doing the job; it's the inside of the person. When you look at the color outside, you don't know what the color is inside until they react, and you don't know what's in there until they react. So how, for Pete's sake, are you going to know people by looking at what color they are? That's a hot one.

Can you imagine that individuals who are well-equipped with degrees from all kinds of different universities and all kinds of professionals such as doctors, lawyers, and scientists, would go around and cast judgment on people because of the color of their skin? Boy is that an insult to your intelligence. That questions your intellectual ability. Who cares about what color you are? Who cares about what nationality you are? What doesn't count is what color the person is. What do they have on the inside? A better community? Do they have better neighborhood support? Better spirit, or the Spirit of God? Do they have the intelligence for progress? All of this is on the inside. You can't see it, because you are hung up on the color on the outside. Is that smart? Well, if that is smart, I'm pretty dumb.

One thing we all know is that our community doesn't have to be what it is. To change it, we have to change. We have to sit down and talk to each other be honest with each other, and admit that we are our own problem. The policemen can't help us, because we do not give them the true evidence. We will not support them. We caused the jails and the prisons to overflow, because the policemen were tied up with one crime that was committed in our community. While they are questioning everyone in our community about one crime, they could be going somewhere else and solving crimes instead of wasting time and money asking us, "What did you see?" We didn't see anything, because we don't want to get involved. See the damage we are doing? You see the cost that is unnecessary and which we are bringing upon our own government, our own community, and our own selves? You see the problems that we are causing? The money that is being spent? The time that is being spent? They are wearing themselves out when we could just speak a word and say, "Yes, we saw it." We could tell the policemen how tall he is, what he looks like, what he was driving. We could say, "Yes it's my nephew, my relative, my son, my husband, or my wife." Yes, that's it. It's settled. Go to the next case.

The thieves will have to get a job; the criminals will have to move. Lives will be saved. We'll become better people and better communities, because the thieves will have nowhere to hide. We won't have to worry about what's behind our house, because our neighbors will keep us informed. We won't have to worry if anyone is going to break into our house while we are away, because the neighbors are at home. Protection is always there. The government will have to close some of it jails, because the crime will be down. Our young people can make something out of their lives. They can look and understand that they have to prepare themselves for an honest living, because all loopholes are closed. All darkness becomes light, because our neighbors have turned light into the dark shadows of night. It closes the path to your back door. All these are closed. He has to look elsewhere to survive in the world in which he lives.

The problem is in our home. The problem is the failure in our neighborhoods, with our neighbors and with our protection of one another. Our truthfulness and concern about each other is our understanding that when we build our community, we are building ourselves. When we help others to be strong, that means we are strong enough to do it, and that will make us stronger. When we do the right thing for others, we are automatically saving ourselves, number one. You want to be happy? Be a part of someone else's happiness. You want your life to be a drag? You don't want to feel like a snob forever. Try to help someone be better. You can be only what you help other to be. If that's you, then you want to see it in others. When we see something great, we want only to see it in ourselves. It cannot remain great. But anything worth anything, we want to see it produce. If we feel our children are good, let them associate with others. Then, they can help make others the same way. You don't want to be a good person in a world all by yourself. You don't want to be the only one who can be trusted in your community.

Your children can hate, and if you bring them up to hate, they will. They will be those kind of people. If you teach them to love, they will be those kind of people. But it's what you plant in their minds and in their hearts. They can't be anything more than what is planted in them. There are things that we experience throughout our adulthood. That is simply because of what people are taught from their youth, from their birth up. There are some white people who hate black people, not because they have done anything or they have any reasons for not liking them, but because they are black. That's no reason at all. The color has never been the person. You get your car the color you want, or you paint your house the color you want, but you don't live in the paint. You don't call that paint your house; it's just the color. The house and the car are behind the paint, so that is nonsense. On the other hand, you have black people who hate white people for no reason at all. Then they go back and say, "You know, I have a great grandfather who had them under slavery." Well, we read about that, and we know that it is true, but we are not under slavery. We haven't been slaves. We read about it, but we don't exactly know what being a slave is like. We don't have to go into slavery to see ugliness in any man. We have men who have been free all of their lives, and have gotten what their heart has desired for all of their lives, but you can't tell them about their actions. The way some of them act, they haven't been exposed to anything positive, and they don't have anything. They are just full of hate. I cannot hate people because I read about things that happened hundreds of years ago when my people were under slavery. Israel was under slavery for a long time, and they are some of the greatest people on the earth today. They are not looking down and talking about what our forefathers did and what they didn't do. They are doing what it takes for them to make a better life for themselves now, which is good sense. That's being thankful for today, and not trying to live all over again.

Some of my best friends are white, and I wouldn't have it any other way. And I feel that I am a friend to some of the white people who know me. I'm talking about personal friends, who are the same regardless of my own color. A friend is a friend not a color. It's the principle, the intelligence, and that gives us reason to live together in a world in which we are trapped. We have to stay here whether we like it or not. These people are better if they are taught early and are not being fed all of the hate and wrong—where the child will come and rob you of your opportunities in the beautiful world in which you live. A man is a man.

I have relatives and children and neighbors who I love, but I don't want them to become my governor or my president. I don't want them as my representative representing me. I don't want color. I want a man. I don't want color and looks. I want a woman, if you are going to represent me. True representation is not color or something that doesn't mean anything to anyone. Let's be realistic about life. It's not pertaining to the betterment of life. I don't care how you rate it, that doesn't make it anything except what it is already. If our world is going to be better, it is going to be better by what we plant in the lives of our children.

We have to extend our community. We have to plant a community. We have to plant a government. We have to plant anything life requires that is dealing with the lives of human beings who have to come through the mysterious life of God, and we do it like God says. If you want better government, do what God says. Do it like he says. If you want better families, let the Lord live there with you. Let His church be in your home and not just in the house of God. He can make us better people. He can make us people who know how to appreciate being whoever He made us.

If you want a better president, raise one. If you want a better governor, raise one. What do you expect? How are you going to get it? If you don't want the governor of your state, then how are you going to get one? If you don't want him to feel like giving everybody a gun, then raise a good one. Raise a governor who will have a better insight into the safety of the lives of people and to make people better instead of worse.

Anyone knows that a gun can make any good person bad. A gun will change you from where you would normally walk away from the situation to the place where you create a crime instead. Guns change people. I'm talking about good people. And putting a gun in everybody's hand is not going to stop the criminal. A good person cannot outshoot a criminal. He doesn't have the heart or nerve to do it. You don't fight fire with fire. You have never seen the firefighters coming to put out a fire and bringing fire, and their truck is on fire and their ladder is on fire. That's common sense.

You don't fight hate with hate. The whole business will fall down. You get that which conquers hate. Love conquers hate, so if you don't want hate, get love. Let love work.

Whatever your name, God has a remedy. If you don't like lies, tell the truth. It's just as simple as that. If you want to be loved, love somebody. If you want to live in hate in the hate system, and the hate storm, just practice hating somebody. If you want better government, raise it. If you want to improve your community, raise it. Children are born and trained. They are not hypocritical, and not wanting them to receive all types of degrees so they can render services to their fellow men is disgusting!

Why do you want to learn about the planets when you know nothing about the world in which you live? How can you be satisfied with such a small stroke of love? Can only love only your family and a few friends but hate the entire nation? That's hypocritical. If you want to love, become a part of it.

Whoever you are, be that person, and plan for the results of it. If you are going to live by the truth, accept Christ in your life. He is the truth. If you are going to live by robbing, be a professional. Don't fill up the jails with people who shoplift—people who go to jail for ten years for stealing a pack of cigarettes. You are not on either side. You are not a robber. You are not a citizen. You prove to be nothing. If you are going to be a liar, be a professional liar. Go to school. Be in the media, which, in my opinion, is known for lying. If the plane falls, and fifty people are killed, the media is going to say that it was fifty-five. I think news is always going to be told differently than what it really is, but people are making a living out of it.

What's the use of going to hell for nothing. If you are going to be a liar, try to live as one for the short time you live. If you don't live right, you're going to hell for wrong living and wrong doings. It's just as simple as that. Be a lawyer, live by your nontruths. Yes, I know what the critics are going to say. The lawyers work on the truth sometimes, but other times they work on a lie as if it were the truth. They are not all that way, but it happens. That's their line of business. They're making a living out of it; they're prospering from it.

When, in your ignorance, you start being silly, you start doing silly things. You are going to take someone's life for a gallon of gas or a pack of cigarettes. That doesn't make any sense; that's crazy. You're absentminded. You don't see any use for yourself in the world or where you are. You value nothing. A human being should see something good about himself. I'm trying to get you to see what will become of people if they are not born at the proper time, to the proper family, and discipline is not applied to train them in the right direction. You don't have to be trained to be a fool. You don't have to be trained to be nothing. You don't have to train to be any kind of liar. Of course, to be a professional liar, you have to train for it. If you want to be nothing, you don't have to go to school to be nothing. Just live. Any man who aims at nothing never misses his target.

The mind. With what is the mind filled? The mind of a child? I think the guy who invented computers he must have patterned himself after a child. Do you want to know what comes up on the screen of a child's life? It's what is fed into it. Whatever is fed into it, you press the button, and the answer appears in reality. Whatever you want to appear on the screen of the child, when the opportunity happens, it will come out. Do you want to know how to respect and how to enjoy the good things out of life? You appreciate them and feed them into the minds of the children. When this happens, we can feel the change even if the change is not made in our own lives. We can go from this world believing that a change is under way.

Let's not turn our back, look the other way, pretend it doesn't exist when the blood is running down the streets in our largest cities. Our boys and girls are away from home. They are in jails with bars on the windows and doors, and we are living at home with bars on our windows and doors. There are prisons in the cities, and we're in jails in our own homes.

I think this situation is reason enough, because you're afraid of your own son. His mind is torn up. He's so dangerous and mixed up, he's like a walking time bomb. He will blow off your head just like anyone else's. Don't tell me we don't have any reason to take a turn for the better. Don't tell me we don't have anything to consider. When this condition rises up in this young man, it doesn't make any difference to him who he kills—mother, father, neighbor, anyone—as long as somebody dies.

Don't tell me we don't have anything to think about or anything to which to turn If ever there was a time we needed to turn to the Lord and say, "We're sorry. We have done wrong. We have failed you," it is now. "You have allowed us to live in a million dollar home, but we have done wrong. You gave us a home and children to live in the home, but they don't mind. They prefer to sleep in the street. They prefer to sleep under bridges and under garbage piles. They prefer to sleep in the crack houses."

We have a lot to consider. We have a lot of reasons why we should come together, sit down, and talk about the case. Hear the minister. Hear the missionaries. They are trying to tell you something. They are talking more about Heaven. They are telling you that it can be pretty good when you live, if you just let God move in with you. Let Him come in. Let Him direct your mind as to what to do. We've made this place a mess. We turned the world upside down without Him. We went against Him. We didn't follow His instructions.

Ministers are so disgusted today. We preach the Word of God to our people. We teach them what the Lord says, and when we watch their reactions, we can't see anything that we have preached. The things you see are that people are doing badly. They didn't learn that from preaching. There are home failures; they didn't learn that from preaching. They may have learned that from not having preaching, but they didn't get it from preaching. The Gospel doesn't teach that kind of life, those kind of actions, and that kind of fruit. You didn't learn to be a murderer from hearing the Gospel. You didn't learn to be a hater from hearing the Gospel. That's not Gospel teaching. Selfishness and self-righteousness—you feel as if you are the only person in the world. You didn't learn that from preaching. You learned that from somewhere else. Why don't you practice what you have heard being preached? Why don't you demonstrate in your lives and in your actions some of the good things that you have heard being preached?

We can wake up in the morning to a beautiful day, look each other in the face, and not say good morning. You didn't learn that from preaching. The Gospel doesn't teach that kind of thing. You want the world for your children, but you want the garbage pails for your neighbor's children. The Gospel doesn't teach that. The Gospel say, "Do unto others as you would have them do unto you."

You're shaking your finger at each other saying, "What goes around comes around." Don't tell me we don't have reasons to stop. Don't tell me we have the answer. Don't tell me man can run around and tell you he can make all the corrections.

Fire the people who have the know-how, the ability, and the experience to carry on and do good things for the country, good things for your community, and for your church. Then you get someone who knows nothing, has been nowhere, has seen nothing, and is doing nothing, and you want him in office. Life just doesn't come that way. The teaching of God says for old men to teach the young men and old women to teach the young women. Teach them at home. Correct their mistakes at home. Teach them proper behavior at home. Let them know how important their behavior is in life. Teach them the way that they should go. Teach them respect. Teach them that every parent is their parent when they are wrong. Teach them they have to behave as well at home as they do when they are not at home. Prepare them to help build a new community. Prepare them not to fight or destroy. Tell them they cannot do it by themselves. Tell them they cannot build a life by themselves. Tell them we are created to live together. Together we stand and divided we fall. Tell them to learn. Tell them to learn by listening. If they fail to listen, they fail to learn. Tell them not to look at people and judge them by the color of their skin or their national origin but by the contents of their minds and hearts. Tell them to know those people, they must know the qualities themselves. You measure good with good. When you add good and good together, it equals good. You don't add good and good and get a bad answer. Good follows good, and bad follows bad. You strive to be the person you want to be and should be. When you do that, you can be that person. But you can't be both. You can't be right and wrong at the same time. You can't be good and bad at the same time. You can't love and hate at the same time. You have to be one or the other. It takes all the qualities and ingredients to make that—just like everything else.

The Lord put us together like the cooks put the cakes together.

The name of the cake doesn't make the cake, it takes the ingredients on the inside to make it. It's not always just the right ingredients, you also must have the proper communication. You can't dump the ingredients into a pile. You must work the ingredients in at the proper place and the proper time.

You cannot make a baby become a man overnight. It doesn't matter how smart he may be. He hasn't matured yet. It takes time. That's why you are approximately seventeen or eighteen years of age before you get out of high school. It takes time. You can't overload the mind of the students by trying to do it overnight; knowledge has to be blended in, day by day, class by class.

We have true evidence that when the home fails, it has effects everywhere else. When the home fails, the community fails. When the home fails, the state fails. When the home fails, the school, the Church, and the government, all fail, because from the home comes all walks of life. These different departments depend upon what comes from the home. We have to go back to the home. First, we have to acknowledge that the problem is there. We have to go back and start all over again—change from this fast life, from this rushing time to go back and recognize time is not ours. Slow the pace and deal with where the problems lie.

Some way and somehow communities are born. Schools, churches, and the entire function of our civilization are born. They must be born on the same order that God had planned for them to be. We have to let God be God and man be man. Let man be the helpless creature that he was born to be, or the nobody he was born to be and to look to his creator, God, for what God would have him to be. We cannot make very much of ourselves; we can only add to what we are. Life comes from the inside and depends upon what comes out. What comes out will depend on what is on the inside. The issues of life come from the inside. If the inside is not right, it cannot come out right. The home plays the major role, because it is the beginning. We're born into this world with nothing. We're born depending on somebody to share with us the right purpose and the right direction, to teach us, to show us, and to bring us up in the right way. If this is not done, it is impossible to have a safe community.

It is impossible to have the kind of men who brought about the kind of world in which we live and the kind of government to keep and to continue to build the kind of democracy that would give people the kind of know-how and the opportunity to make great investments into the land where they live. That means the best is to be recognized by those who depend upon the ability of others. Isn't it sad that when we find the people who have the experience and who have given their lives to building a country like the United States, people are screaming on every corner that they are no good. They are in office too long. They make their careers there. Who would deny that kind of investment if they make their career building a great country, which they have shown by making America the richest country and the most powerful country on earth. And you are going to reject that. You are going to feel as if someone who has no experience and who just got here can come in and replace those kinds of people? But you know, when we lose our sense of direction, we lose the proper function of our mind. We speak before we think. We fall into the pit before we realize there is a pit there. Simply for this reason, no one can become a genius overnight. No one can be very much overnight. But what we can be is to be thankful for those who have suffered and brought us from a very long way. Be thankful that we have been able to replace the men who have given us such a great country and such convenience while all the things that we have become accustomed to doing. We refuse to fall under the level at which we are now living. But instead of appreciating the comfortable conditions in which we live, we count them as nothing and scream for more.

Look at the home today. We don't have time to appreciate what we have accumulated among ourselves. We have replaced the communication and love for one another with things. Many homes today have four and five televisions and not one friend.

Our home has become a boring place, we say, with all kinds of TV, stereos. It's boring because we feel we can go through life without people, without neighbors, or without just down-to-earth conversations and that our minds can relax and concentrate on life as a whole. Nothing can replace neighbors. Nothing can replace communication among people. We are suffering because of noncommunication. We live next door to people and don't even know their names. We live next door to each other and we can hardly see each other going in and out. There is no communication, no respect for one another.

Our homes have become dreadful places to go. Most men would rather not see the sun go down, because they refuse to go home. Home has become a desert place in our minds, because we have moved in a world all by ourselves. Everything we need is on the outside, and we are trying to survive with the emptiness that is in our minds and in our homes.

What is there for the children to do? What is it to fill their lives and plant ideas about communities, professions, and all of the other things that should be planted into the minds of our children? When the parents are bored, the children are bored and restless. They need to become involved and to communicate with each other, to learn together, play together, study together, grow up together, understand each other, love each other, walk with each other, and become stronger men and women together. That tie will make a better world and community. That tie will block the road of thieves and robbers who penetrate our communities. When you have strong boys and girls who will not accept any packages or ideas from strangers, the strangers who ride by and kidnap would not have that road to travel, because the girl and boys on that road would be too smart for that. They would be watching over each other. Isn't it sad today that a child can walk outside the door, get kidnapped, and nobody sees anything.

THE SECOND INSTITUTION: THE SCHOOL

The second institution is the school. The child is making a transition from the home to the school. The question is, is this child prepared to enter into this important stage of life? He has the new jeans, sneakers, pencils and paper, but do these items qualify him to enter into this new life experience, which is the school? Has this child been told about this new life? Was he told of the transition that would take the place between the child and parents from the previous institution? Did they tell him about the new relationship that would take place in their lives and that the person who would fill the space of the parents would be the teacher.

Tell children how important teachers are. Tell them that this person only can fill the emptiness in their lives, and complete their lives in dealing with the future. Have you told them they should love their teacher as they do their mother? Did you tell them the teacher has the answer for completing their lives in a human society on this earth, on which their future largely depends? Did you tell them that obedience is the key step to their success? Did you tell them that this teacher will spend more daylight hours with them than any other person in their lives? Did you tell them that peace and harmony must prevail for them to be successful in their school days? Did you tell them it's important to listen to what the teacher is saying, and to cooperate with their teachers as they share their experiences and to give them the answers to their future that they do not have? Did you tell them that all their dreams and plans would depend upon their staying in school and working with their teachers, or did you tell them that all of their hopes and all of their dreams of what they want to be in life or how far they want to go in life would depend upon the time they spend with this person? Did you tell them that the teacher loves them and that their lives have been dedicated to them? Or, did you forget to explain that?

By forgetting the ingredients of their future, you told them different. You told them they didn't have to do what the teacher told them to do or listen to the teacher if they didn't want to. The question is, if they won't listen to the teacher, to whom are they going to listen? Parents you're not there. Even if you were there, you would be unable to give them what is required at this time in their lives. So, why are they in school? If you have all these answers, why send them to school? If you are better equipped than the teachers to meet their future needs through education, why are you not here in this second institution?

Did you tell you children that the teacher would have to please them, and get along with them, or should the children get along with and obey the teacher? Are the children prepared to go through a smooth transition? Did you give them some pointers in their lives so it won't be a problem for the teachers to continue where you left off—to continue with the building of their lives in the world, in the community, or in the government. Or, are the children filled with many conjunctions in their lives unnecessarily—to destroy them before they get started.

Do you understand that you have the first choice? You, as parents, do you realize that you have the first choice to mold this child's mind and attitude to receive that which is yet to come? Did you not know that this life is being sent into this institution not to be born, but to live, to mature, and to be prepared for the next steps in life? Did you realize you cannot be the parents at home and that the teacher sheds tears over the disasters that come from the home? Did you realize that there is a precious life and a future that is at state?

It requires the very best from all people who are involved to give their best for the future of this child. The child should have some preparation, because God spoke first about home. He spoke first by saying, "Train up a child in the way he should go: and when he is old, he will not depart from it." (Proverbs 22:6.) The teacher can only add to what comes from the home. If the right direction is planted in the minds of the children, teachers can be a guide to better things. But to spend their time trying to first plant in the minds of the children the way it should go, instead of being able to begin with where they should go and how they are going to get there, will cause a defect in the children's future.

Train them. Train them how to be thankful, and train them to say, "Thank-you." Train them how to say, "Yes sir, yes ma'am, or "thank you." And if you parents teach them how to say it, the teachers will teach them how to spell it or use it. Teach them that intelligence is required in their future. Teach them that when they leave home, they're not going among animals but among human beings. Also, teach them to look up instead of looking down, to come with an open mind, and to seek and to learn instead of exploding the things that are unnecessary or unwelcome in this great institution. So, demonstrate our successes or our failures by the behaviors and attitudes of the children.

When we look at the child, what do we see? Do we see a possibility for some great position, some strength, some places to be filled by some professional job holder, some future company worker, operator, banker—all these things that make up our society? Do we see that in the children, or do we see jailhouses, prisons, dope possessors, or graveyards? What do we see in them? What have we planted in them?

In this institution, which is the school, teachers can only improve what comes from the first institution, which is the home. If you send good to the school, you can get back better. If you send bad to the school, you'll get back worse. So the giving is important, but the taking is reality. It is for us to decide. The home training cannot be a no.

There's another scripture that says, "Even a child is known by doings, whether his works be pure, and whether it be right." (Proverbs 20:11.) What reactions children demonstrates in school, it's very well understood, are what was planted in them. What is planted in their minds comes to action. That's what learning will do. Learning will wake up what's in you. It will not reach out and put something else into the children, but it will only bring out of the children what's in them.

When the school meets these problems, the unruly children with bad attitudes, who are desperate in hate, selfish, and have violent minds come out when they go to school. Isn't it sad that people have to suffer these things, and they are not responsible for them? Isn't it sad that we bring this interference to the school from our home to interrupt other students? Isn't it sad when we look and talk to other students in the school and hear and see so much hate coming out of the small children, who have come from the home? Their attitude comes from the home.

We need to think about your problems in life as revealed in school by your children. The children did not ask for hate or this bad behavior themselves. Where did they get it? They got it from home. And it's unfair to the teacher, to the institution, and to the community for you to contaminate the minds of the children that will hurt other children. Let's think about it. It violates the principle of the Word of our Lord. It goes on the Scripture, which is inspired by God and given by Solomon, that says, "Foolishness is bound in the heart of a child; but the rod of correction shall drive it far from him." (Proverbs 22:15.) Now, this doesn't mean to beat the children to death, but it does mean to discipline them. You don't abuse the children, but it comes by sometimes that they do need chastisement in whatever form the chastising may be.

No one spends a lifetime trying to correct one situation. Using straps or spanking will not have to occur, when the children recognize they don't own the school or the teacher. Once they realize they have to fall in line, like all of the other students, and obey the rules and the regulations, that discipline is over. But if the word, the holy word, says that discipline is essential to the child, who are we to say different? The Lord knows more about the human life, because he's the one who made us. He knows what we requires. He's the one who made it possible to have these institutions, teachers, and ways to build our communities, homes, churches, and governments in the lives of people. He's the one who prepared it. Therefore, certainly, He rejects our way of thinking, because our way of thinking can never compete with the thinking of God.

Right will have to master wrong in anyone's life. Truth will have to master lies in anyone's life. Progress will have to master failure in anyone's life. Good will have to master bad in anyone's life. Success will have to take the front row over failure in anyone's life in order for God's world, for God community, to be blessed by God. I think we should realize our way is not God's way. We must realize that we can have many suggestions, but they don't always have to be the answer. I think we are more interested in what we think and what we feel rather than what are facts. We seem to minimize the purpose in bringing up our children. When we do this, we minimize our children, and we minimize our state, government, and our entire world. All the good thing you want out of the land, out of the job, and out of the world, must come through the life of children, no other way. They cannot be born and grow up automatically in their own way and accomplish things. A baby knows nothing about community, nothing about a government, nothing about anything. He is only a life that God has provided for us to plant a kind of community, a kind of church, or the home that we decide to have by His leadership. All of that is broken. All of that is destroyed, and we suffer from it. It's dangerous now. It's dangerous in the lives of our children. The children are murdering their parents simply because that's how we have reared them.

Have we really prepared the children for this institution? Have we told them the things that they really need to know? Some people think that their children are all truth; they never lie. I can't see why. All of us have lied; some of us are still lying. The children will lie to take the pressure of themselves. When our children realize we will stand up and support them when they are wrong, turn our backs on the teachers, and break up the relationship that the teacher is trying to get with the children, we make the teacher an enemy in the minds of the children. That's hypocritical. That hypocrisy brings disturbance, bad feelings between the child and the teacher. And the children must remain in school; they must remain there. Your children must remain until the time has expired, and you are going to help them destroy with that which they have to deal. We have them hating to go to school and hating to see the morning come but glad to see the weekend come and glad to see vacation time come so they can be out of school.

I enjoy, many times, talking with young people when they say, "I'm sorry school is out," and "I can't wait until school begins. I'm bored, I don't have any of the challenges that I would have at school." That means progress. That means these young people will reach their goals and be able to move from this institution and be ready to move up instead of moving down.

Are we the cause of this? Are we the cause of our children hating to go to school? Are we the cause of them not having a relaxed mind, a challenging mind? Are we responsible for that? If we are not, then who? Let's think about it. They leave our home pleased in the morning. By the time they reach the school, they are bitter, and they are that way until the bell rings for the day. Then they began to leap and jump because they are ready to leave this place.

Can you imagine hating this place and being ready to leave the place that's preparing them for life? Can you imagine all of this simply because the mind is filled with the wrong things? I believe we should think of the child's mind as always being a computer. He was a computer even before the computer system was invented. Whatever you feed into the mind is going to soon appear on the screen. When the button of life is touched, whatever you fed in, will soon come out.

When we rear our children with hate, hate doesn't have any

respect for parents. It doesn't draw the line. Hate will hate everybody. Hate will hate itself. It's hard to understand. Sometime we can teach our children to hate and try to have the mind to direct their hate. You can't train a child to hate a person, to hate black only. It's impossible. If a person hates black, they hate whites. They hate the same thing. Hate is not color blind. Hate will hate anybody, and when you plant hate in your child, somewhere along the line, that hate is going to turn on you. Have you learned? Even the things that we have talked about you have heard, but you have ignored it. You have heard your minister preach it. You have heard your minister teach it and your missionary teach it. You have heard it over and over, but you don't take heed to it. You want it your way.

Think about it. How can you live in God's world and have your way? You didn't create anything. The land you claim to be yours, you didn't make. Out of all that we have made or invented, nobody can make land. All the land that will ever be is already made. The sun, the moon, and the rain—all of these things belong to God, are operated by God, and were sent to us by the Lord. We own nothing. We brought nothing into this world, and we will carry nothing out. God lends to us what we see around us. He lends it to us. If you bought land, God didn't sell it to you. The legal system sold it to you. God's land is not for sale. The land does not belong to the legal system. Lawyers just transact the business that they have made themselves.

If we teach, whatever we teach is going to have a bearing on us. If we teach hate, it's going to show up in our lives.

How did we come to disgrace our training and this institution, this school of learning? Can you imagine that all the scientists, and all the lawyers and all the wise people we have in this world—people able to fly planes, able to go to the moon, etc.—and we don't know that God can destroy all that our eyes can see, and He is doing it? America knows a little, very little, about wars. Many wars were in other places, and many generations know nothing about wars in America. They only know about fighting and supporting wars in other places. Do you think that this causes people to outsmart other people? We become the God-fearing people, and, therefore, we're not being destroyed by other wars or people coming in. We're destroying ourselves.

How are we destroying ourselves? Through ignorance, but not about the great things. We're not ignorant about going to the moon or other great things. We're ignorant concerning the small things within our selves. We don't think much about ourselves. When you can't love and respect human beings, then your love is useless. Automobiles don't need your love. Your house doesn't need your love. Highway systems, buses, and trains don't need your love. Human beings do. They are what love is for. You use these things. You are grateful for these things, grateful that they were created in our lifetime. But when you can't love and enjoy people, your life is miserable. Your life is miserable. Is it smart for you to ride down the street in your Cadillac car meet a man walking, and you hate him? You love the Cadillac, but you hate the human being. Isn't it sad that you can bring up children and educate them in every field with all kinds of degrees and never feel the degree of love? They are blind to love.

What makes such a difference? What makes such a difference in color? Color is not a man. The man is not just color. The man is only covered with color. It's not the color of your house in which you live. You live behind the color and you're going to come and burn the house down because it's black. Boy, that's a hard one. We can do some strange things. Then we wonder what is happening to our nation, our country. We are slowly destroying ourselves. At a time, when we are concentrating on this work, there are churches throughout the country being burned down, houses of God being burned down. What kind of sense can you find in burning down the house of God? Now we don't know what kind of people they are, but you can believe they are driving automobiles, something that is convenient. They're living in homes. They are enjoying the sunshine and the rain. Most likely they have bank accounts. They have what everyone else has. But they can find nothing of gratitude to do but to burn down the house of God.

How empty-minded can you be? Is this the gratitude for your enjoyment? Is this what you get from the rain on your crops and on your lawns, the sunshine everyday, and all of the convenient things that you have? This is the only way you can say thank you? To burn down where people go to worship and to thank the Lord? How do you think this country stands it? What do you think would happen if all the worship places were destroyed and all the people who worship stopped worshipping? Don't you know America would be another Africa? Children would be dying. They would be starving to death in their mother's arms, perishing without any guns being fired or from any accident, just dying from starvation. If all the people stop worshipping and the houses of God burned down, how long do you think this country would stand? This country's prosperity comes from people who worship and praise God, not from your stupidity and not from your inability to return any kind of thankfulness to God or anyone else? No mercy is shared from your life. With some people, a human being is no more than a tree. We're suppose to be civilized people. I guess that makes you free, makes you justified in doing whatever you want to do because you call yourself radical or some kind of society. You're sad. You're almost to sad too enjoy such a life as you are living. What happened? From where did you learn that? From where did you get that idea? Did you get it from the school? Did you get it from the home? Believe me, you didn't get it from the Lord. That's the devil's work.

We're living in the midst of hatred and self-destruction. Men are supposed to be smart in a country that leads the land, the earth, the so-called power, the beauty, and the prosperity. They are doing their best to destroy it all. The government and the democracy that brought them here, they are doing a good job in destroying it. They are turning people against themselves, because we are the government. They found a corner in one place to cast the blame. The blame for what? We experience a few years of high living. We have gotten to a certain level of living. Our lifestyle has become higher than we can handle. We don't have enough common sense to back off. Instead of putting a limit or level on our spending, we go higher and higher. Men promise you will have more. More of what? Listen, we have more now than we have ever had. We're living better than we ever have before. That's why we have turned from God. If you can't live with two or three cars in the driveway, get rid of them. Get rid of them. Get rid of them. If you have three, get rid of two of them. You can't ride in more than one at a time anyway. If you can't live up to it, give it up. Don't fight or destroy each other because you can't find a way to pay your debt. You complain about how much you are in debt, when you should complain about the stupid war games in which our country is engaged. What about your war game with yourself? If you can't handle five televisions, settle for one. You can't watch more than one television at a time anyway. If you can't handle a telephone in every room of your house, and one for your pocket, just have one. That way everybody will be happy. Don't turn people against each other and blame them for your not having more. More, more, more. We have more now than our grandparents could ever dream of; they would have no way of knowing that the country would be what it is today. This should be the happiest place in the world. As far as prosperity, as far as comfort, we have nothing to worry about. Usually when you have nothing to worry about, you will find something to hate. You have to do something.

Togetherness less is defeating the destruction. Unity is strength. Where there is unity, there is strength. A country or kingdom cannot stand divided against itself. Who cares what color you are?

What difference does it make? Your character, your intelligence, your attitude is what counts. What difference does it make where you eat or drink as long as you have an appetite? That's the most important thing about it. The man who owns the supermarket has a chance to eat when or wherever he wants as long as he has an appetite. Appetites don't come from the supermarket. Taste doesn't come from the supermarket.

In all of your getting, if you don't get what God graciously gives you, the other means nothing. Clear out your house. Get rid of all of your beds, and get water beds, king size beds, or whatever you want. When you get all of these beds, from where will the sleep come? Can you make sleep? Can you buy sleep? No. Without the sleep that God gives us, what good is the bed? What good is the bed? The whole world is crazy over nothing for nothing. It's not by doing something. We don't know why. Why can't men get along in a world together. Why do schools and churches have to suffer from the fallout of stupidity. That's exactly what it is.

If you are not satisfied with the world God gave you, why don't you move out. Don't try to live in His world and leave Him on the outside. You can't do that. We bring destruction upon ourselves. It's sad to think about what we are headed for and will bring upon ourselves. Not any other country. Not any other people. We are doing it to ourselves.

It is frightening that there is a possibility of blowing ourselves up trying to blow up other people. There are gas lines everywhere, all kinds of explosives everywhere, and some mindless person is going around setting off explosives. Where did they learn it? This institution is meant to prepare lives for the better. Why won't somebody tell somebody that life does not consist of that behavior under the rules of the Lord, under the rules of God.

We make ourselves enemies toward each other, and any time that you can't love, you automatically hate. You don't have to go to school to hate. You are just not taught to love. You don't practice love. You will automatically hate. Your children don't have to learn how to do wrong, just don't teach them how to do right. Children don't have to learn how to be ignorant, just don't teach them to be smart. It automatically comes, and when you find people existing and exalting on the outside of good sense, you know what's wrong with them. There is no way for us to correct the situation until we stop and start all over again.

Where do you start? At home. With whom do you start? The children being born, or the children who are born and who are being filled with the future. That's what has happened to our schools. Our schools are planning the future. The schools need all of the help they can get. They need these three institutions to come together. Let us claim our faith. Everybody wants to claim the good part; everybody wants to claim the accomplishments. If you are in on them you have a right to, but you should also claim the faith.

So, the home, the school, and the church have failed, and the only alternative is that these three institutions come together, and say, "We have failed." It's very difficult to do it now, because we have lost our control. The courts and the government have taken control of the home. That should have never happened. They took control of the school; it shouldn't have to be. The church is standing with nothing to work with. This is the situation. If you are not prepared in the homes or schools, it gives the church very little to do. The biggest thing that you have left for the minister to do is bury the dead and pray for mercy. We pray as if it is some kind of made-up idea, or many people see praying as a good luck charm, like a rabbit's foot, or some kind of headache pill that you keep fastened up in a box and open it only when your head is hurting.

I remember some time ago, when Desert Storm was raging and war was going on. They had sent out calls to every city hall, police station, and fire station. Everybody was to meet and pray for the *storm* to end. And when the *storm* ended, they bought a lot of alcoholic beverages to celebrate. They prayed to God to end the *storm*, and when the *storm* was over, they got drunk. We can do some very stupid things. If that is smart, I want to be dumb. It was a short war, and when it was over, the men were able to come home. The same people began celebrating and getting drunk about the war being over. There was not enough courtesy, and not enough thanksgiving, not enough knowledge about what they were doing to call the crowd back and say, "Let's praise the Lord; let's thank him because He heard our prayer." But no, we get drunk. In other words, "Lord you have done it; we don't need you anymore. We want to feel good, and we don't want your spirit. We don't want your grace. We don't want your joy. We want something to drink that will make us feel like we want to feel." This describes the kind of people we are. This is the kind of thanksgiving we give. This is the way we express ourselves when things are well with us. When things are down, we want everybody to pray. When it looks up, we want everybody to stay out of our way. When we're down, when we have storms in the community, and when hurricanes come, we have shelters, and everybody comes from all directions. They lay together and eat together as long as the storm is going on, but when the storm is over, everybody wants to go back home and be who they were before. These games are not good games to play. They not only look stupid, they smell stupid, because reaction is there—ungrateful, unthankful.

What can we do? Instead of training the children to get them ready to enter into this other institution, what happens. We contaminate their minds. We have taught them how to be silly—not smart, but silly. Don't listen to the teacher. Don't do what the teacher says to do. You don't have to sit there, you can walk out. You have more students today who are just walking out of class, just walking out.

They don't want to hear what you are saying. They say, "I hate the teacher; I don't like the teacher." Isn't that something? I want to tell you something children, if you can't like your teacher, you can't like your own mother, whatever *like* is. If you can't love your teacher, you can't love your mother. Love is not blind. Love will fall in its proper place, and love will love anyone.

We're not quite ready. All of those who succeed through this institution and move to a better life are the ones who have planned and are prepared at home. There are some who will listen and get on the right track, but they will always have something missing. It will be an incomplete life, because every time a child is set back, he or she cannot overcome it. This will leave a vacancy in his or her life. Isn't it sad that we claim to be loving people, and we claim to love our home, love our school, and love our children, but we show such little support? We uphold wrongdoing. We uphold low moral conduct. Many times we are lifted up in our pride. Our pride is too cheap to live. Our pride is too sick; it will made you sick if you only think about who you are and what you are.

The most independent and disturbing people in this situation are the people who are not working. The people who get support from other sources, such as income from the government, are the hardest people to get along with. They don't care about getting along with anyone else. They don't care whether or not their children are good children. They will *curse you out* if you call their attention to certain things. They are not the only ones, but they are some of the worst, some of the worst. They are independent, selfish, and high-minded, (For no reason whatsoever they are independent, thinking that of you are not taking care of me, or you are not doing this for me.) People who build their lives on what somebody is doing for them cannot expect very much out of life. There in no pleasure in living your life on handouts when you can do better. There are some people who need help, need someone to help them.

The Lord has always kept these people among us, because it's a blessing to be able to help somebody. But when people begin to take advantage of it, it's like making plans without a purpose. They become a soul without hope, and feel as if they need no one. I think someone should tell them, everyone needs someone. We must stop and study ourselves, and make a new start, or we will continue downwards. Before you can reach your destiny and find out you are on the wrong road, you have to realize that you are wrong, and headed in the wrong directions.

There's another way we can help. The parents and the teachers have lost touch with each other. There once was a time I can remember when each month there was a meeting between the parent and the teacher. That's no longer the case in a lot of places. They don't know each other. They are supposed to be the closest people in the community—the parents and the teachers—because they are playing the same role in the life of the children. The only time the parents want to go to the school is if they receive some kind of false report, when they wish to state their unpleasant reason, or when they go to defend their children right or wrong, with a useless attitude. That's not good for the children. You need to know each other. You need to talk to each other. You need to discuss the progress or the failure of the children. If the parents and the teachers are not working together, how will they have any accomplishments dealing with the children. Some way, somehow, we need to get together and restore the relationship between with the teachers and the parents. They need to reason together and come together on common grounds to deal with the hurtful situation that is taking place in the lives of our children.

Somehow, we don't seem to have time, or maybe we are guilty. Certainly you don't want to meet with the teacher if you have taught the children unpleasant things concerning the teacher. You don't want to talk, because you are guilty, and you know the children will be honest concerning the things you have taught. Whether they be positive or negative, the children are going to be honest.

Therefore, be mindful what we plant in the mind of the child. Whatever we plant is coming up. Whatever we feed into the mind of that child, when the switch is touched, it's coming to the screen. This can be very embarrassing, or, if we teach the right things, it can be very encouraging. (It's a matter of time, which we think we have a lot of. We think, sometimes, we don't have any, but most of the time, it's wasted on nothing).

I think we get too busy to deal with the problems of life. We have just become too busy. Let us all stop, stop blaming and shaking fingers at each other. We have all failed. the child is the one getting the short end of a beautiful life, and we are coming up short with the problems in the home, the community, the school, and the Church.

Don't leave out government. Our entire country depends upon what happens at home. Everyone from the president to the custodian comes from the home. That's the way it is, and that's the way it's going to be. If the problem is with the home, it's just like the man who hits the home run and circles the bases, but misses first base. He's out. You must touch all the bases. If we have missed our goals, who suffers? We all suffer. The children suffer because they were unable to build their future. We suffer because they didn't accomplish it, and we fall short of being the kind of people it takes. Good citizens, doctors, lawyers, and all kinds of business people come first from the home.

It's been too long that we have sat down and thought the school can handle the problems of the home. It never has; it never will. Churches have been blamed for the downfall of our people. Not so. Until these three institutions come together, the Church cannot exercise its divine mission to reach out and to help. It is one thing that can be a great failure when a person misses the opportunity to grow. The whole situation is summed up by the great Apostle, Paul, who said, "For we know in part, and we prophesy in part. But when that which is perfect is come, then that which is in part shall be done away. When I was a child, I spake as a child, I understood as a child, I thought as a child: but when I became a man, I put away childish things." (1 Corinthians 13: 9-11)

One of the things that can be hurtful throughout life is when children grow up and do not know the transition of times in their lives. Nothing can be so out of place as an adult speaking like a child or understanding like a child. The only way we can prevent this behavior from happening is to have consistency from the home to the school to the Church. The transitions will automatically take place, because the knowledge of the Word of God tells us that if the life and mind is ministered to at the proper time, these different conjunctions will be made within themselves. You have to understand as an adult in order to speak as an adult. But if you understand as a child, you will have to speak as a child. When you speak as a child, and you should be an adult, you don't measure up, and you won't have any support as far as accountability. We need to rear the children when they are children and teach the child when the time comes. We need to make sure they have the proper tools and attention to catch these times in life when the time is right. You cannot replace; you cannot recall back. You are talking about living human beings. You cannot wait until children are teenagers to try and teach them as children, that time has passed. They have begun to mature as adults. They have begun to be men, and the saddest part is when you have a man and he has not been taught. When you look at our government, when you look at our representatives, a lot of them talk like children, and if you listen to them long enough, some of them understand like children. This makes them speak like children. You have to be conscious within yourself and pay attention to what you are saying and doing. It's bad to hold a man's position and speak like a child. Therefore, a child speaks as a child, because he understands as a child. But the time comes when we become men, and we should put away childish things.

It is childish to go around and pull down somebody else to push yourself up. Not only is this behavior childish, it is foolish. Look at people today. They are striving, and spending a lot of money to try to be the top person of the nation, and they are trying to put down the one who is on top today. You just don't get it that way. You grow up by carrying others with you. If you carry others with you, they, in turn, will also keep trying to help carry you. But to grow up by pulling down, you have no foundation when you get there. That's like the people in our political world who take money and sell votes to get people in office or buy votes. (Those who accept owe you nothing when it's over). Anytime someone buys something from you, you are no longer the owner. So if they buy votes from you and they don't do anything in your behalf, they owe you nothing. You have nothing to complain about, they bought it from you.

When you grow up and are trained, when you have taken life step by step, followed every grade, acquired every degree, and made your accomplishment, you don't owe an individual anything. You owe your community, your neighbors, your nation, and your people, because they are the ones who made you what you are.

Thank God for this great man of God who beautifully explained so that young and old could understand. You cannot send a child to do a man's job. You cannot send a man who once was a child but has not taken the steps of a man. Yes, it makes a difference. It makes a difference how you become a man, how you are qualified. It makes a difference whether you can earn a degree or buy one. When you buy a degree, it's just takes part in your ignorance and joins in on the same level. But when you earn a degree, it captures the space of ignorance in your mind.

I, too, can say, "Thank God" When I was a child, I was taught to respect, and to humbly speak as a child. I respected those who supervised me. I thought as a child, I spoke as a child, and my understanding was that of a child. That's why I can tell you today that the importance of life, this community, this world, and this government can be no more than what comes from our intellect, our inner life. If we don't have it, we can't produce it. If it's not there, it can't come from there. A man born rich cannot know how a poor man feels or suffers. He can read about it, but he will never know how he feels. You have to experience the feeling. That's why you have to be a child before you can be a man. A man who becomes a husband before he becomes a man makes people suffer because of it. You must be a man before you become a father. You must be a child brought up in the proper perspective in order to be the kind of man God would have you be. We can praise God and be thankful for all that he put into us and for the courage he gives us in our lives for the betterment of our community and our fellow men. We should keep this in mind and govern ourselves accordingly. Do this, and we will be thankful and proud of each other. Then we can live together in unity and respect. We can also be helpful to each other to make a better community and a better country in which to live.

Remember, we cannot get up by pulling others down. It takes those who are going up to carry us up. So, speak like a man, not as a child. Grow as a child, understand as a child, and know when to put the child away and be a man. God will bless you.

Oh, what a wonderful privilege we have to serve in this capacity of life. We can give so much, we can help so much, and we can love so much. This makes life worth living anywhere, in any community or in any place on God's good Earth. It's good when you are able to enjoy it. You cannot enjoy it without people, without one another. When we learn that, we have learned the joy of living, to respect each other, and how to live together in unity. Where there is peace, there's prosperity. Where there's unity there's strength. Where there are people God, prevails.

God should be the Head of our lives. He is our life. If we accept him on his terms, things will be well with us. Things cannot be well with us until they are well with the people around us. We cannot enjoy the glory of God all alone. We need each other. Night or day, we need each other in this life. If we want to be successful in our lives, we have to do it together—not one by one, not race by race or color by color, but as a human family. We can make our accomplishments together. We can praise God together, because He is the giver of all. He's the God of all. He's the Lord of our lives, the creator, and the maker. He's the one who will call the order in all of our lives sooner or later. That's in His own providence. No man knows the hour or the time that He will come. If we live together, claim it, and contribute enough, we can enjoy the life of eternity through Jesus Christ our Lord in every respect and in every place and time. It belongs to God. Let us stand together, work together, study together, and share each other's burdens.

THE THIRD INSTITUTION:
THE CHURCH

The Church is the spiritual part of life. The Church brings together the knowledge of the previous two institutions, and it can be strengthened by the wisdom of God. We looked at the previous institutions, the home and the school. Now we will look at the Church. We saw that the home failed, The home failed through ignorance, and with the absence of the leadership from God. The school is caught up between the home and the Church. The school is failing because of its handicap. The school is unable to exercise the ability to know how and the purpose for which it is meant, because it has been stripped by the courts, the government, and the home. The Church is failing because of ignorance, and being too independent, too free.

The Church failed because the personnel of the other two institutions failed. It is the personnel who failed. If the personnel fail everything else fails. The parents failed, because they were not following the instruction of God. The school failed, because its personnel are handicapped, stripped of their authority, and unable to exercise their skills. The Church is failing, because the ministers are failing. The ministers have turned away from their divine calling. Many are not called, inspired, or sent from God. And out of it all, out of every affliction of the world, God has worked His plans through man.

There is one thing that God kept to himself; He has chosen His men, inspired them and sent them out to do his will. We have let our God down, and we have failed to stand up for the general principle. Anyone who decides he or she wants to preach and be a minister does so. There are no questions. There is no one to answer to, and no one cares about the action, even among our people. Ministers are responsible for the failure in the church.

When you are not called or sent by God, you have nowhere to go.

You do not have the relationship with God to do what needs to be done. We should be equipped with a vision, and that has already been said: "Where there is no vision, the people perish: but he that keepeth the law, happy is he." (Proverbs 29:18). Most have no vision. They are not seeking. They don't care about a vision. They operate from their own ideas. That's one thing I could never understand. There are men who go out claiming to be men of God. They get a congregation then isolate themselves from districts, state conventions, national conventions, and everything. And people have to believe what the minister says. They don't know if he is right or wrong. How can they know? How can he be right all alone? No questions. The minister doesn't attend anything. He doesn't go to any district meetings. He doesn't go to state conventions, national conventions, or to congress. He just doesn't attend anything. The people are depending on him for their eternity. No one says anything. No one calls and questions him concerning the misuse of privileges that go with the name of the Church. No one says anything. He just goes and leads people anywhere, because he doesn't know where he is going. So how can he lead anyone?

This is happening all over the land. It's given permission by pastors who will ordain these types of ministers. You have some pastors who will ordain anyone. There are more women being ordained now than men. Now, pastors are ordaining women and giving them permission to do something that the Lord didn't tell them to do. This pastor is not fit to hold that office. He's a disgrace to his own calling. We have no such Scripture or experience where Jesus called any women to participate in preaching the Gospel. Nor did the apostles. We have no record of them calling women to preach either. The doctrine of the Church is a doctrine of the apostles, and if the apostles didn't indoctrinate the women of the Church, how can they get to be preachers? How can they pastor? It's sad when men who are known to be leaders, divine leaders, are nearsighted and demonstrate that they are operating totally on their own ideas and to please their own self-righteousness.

Contamination comes in many different ways. Women were not created to preach or to pastor churches. They are not the clean vessels who were accepted by Christ to play such role in the Church of the Living God. The problem in our Church today is that the people are not fed; they are not taught the true Word of God. They are not disciplined in their spiritual lives. The prophets spoke of these types of situations, which point out that we, as ministers, are held responsible for the failure and perishing of our people. One prophet said, "For my people is foolish...they are wise to do evil...." (Jeremiah 4:22) People know how to do evil; we all but teach them how to do evil. We teach them how to separate themselves and make class people out of themselves. Even ministers have their class as—upper class, middle class, low class, or no class at all. They have their popularity, and all of the things that spell no knowledge at all. But they are prepared to do evil. "For my people is foolish, they have not known me; they are Scottish children, and they have none understanding: they are wise to do evil, but to do good they have no knowledge." (Jeremiah 4:22) When people are wise to do evil, it spreads throughout the land pretty fast. They have the know-how and the support by the ones who are leading them. Hosea 4:6 says, "My people are destroyed for the lack of knowledge: because thou has rejected knowledge, I will also reject thee, that thou shall be priest to me: seeing thou hast forgotten the law of thy God, I will also forget thy children." They destroy, because of the lack of knowledge. We don't have to look around for the young people who are being destroyed and who are going to destruction unnecessarily.

Young people are destroying themselves before they start living. Men are not dying fast enough; they are committing suicide. They have no regard for parenting, children, or anyone else. A man loses his head, takes a gun, and blows people's brains out, or his own. All these kinds of things are ignorance, because of the lack of knowledge. These people are unable to understand that life is so beautiful. Life is worth living. If the men of the Church are not feeding the flock with the knowledge of God, people will perish. There is nothing else for them to do but perish. There is nothing else for them to do but destroy themselves.

We must understand that we are held responsible for what we preach, or teach, and certainly for that for which we stand. We must understand that the Lord is going to call and question us, and we must all give an account of our doings. Paul sums it up in Romans 10:1-3: "Brethren, my heart's desire and prayer to God for Israel is, that they might be saved. For I bear them record that they have a zeal of God, but not according to knowledge. For they being ignorant of God's righteousness, and going about to establish their own righteousness, have not submitted themselves unto the righteousness of God."

Most pastors today don't even have a discipline, nor do they use it for the operation, or the biblical truth of their church. Ninety percent of them have written their own bylaws, and that's what it is, bypassing all doctrine and truth to set up your ideas.

Everyone has set the rules and plans of their own congregations, and they operate on their own fancy ideas. People can violate the principles of the Church, curse out everyone in the congregation, go to another church, unite with that church, and no questions are asked. Many people live mostly in the cities and have been a part of nearly every congregation there. Any little thing that happens, such as just get tired of looking at the people, they change congregations. They walk out of the congregation without telling anyone that they are leaving. They walk into the next congregation and don't tell them why they left the last one. These are the kind of bylaws they have cut loose from the biblical operation of the Church. There is no protection for the lives of those who are following. Sometimes you have to help people to do right by calling their actions into question, or their failures or reasons for dropping out. There are very few people in the world today who don't have their names on some role in some congregation. There are many violators, people who have ordained deacons for a lifetime, and most deacons are operating the Church. The Church is being operated as if it were some kind of auction, company, or lumberyard. You name it, and the Church operates in that manner. The people hire the pastor, and they fire him when they get ready. The Holy Spirit is not made known, and the people are not told that he is who appoints the man of God to be the overseer and to feed the flock. Our knowledge is no good to operate God's Kingdom, and as soon as we wake up the better we will be in helping someone else.

The Church is taken for a game, a sporting institution, instead of a divine institution. Pride has taken over. Most of the time, the pastor is leading the way. He wears twelve diamonds on his hand, and he has only ten fingers. That means he sometimes has two rings on one finger. Chains hang all around his neck. He has become a statue instead of a man of God, a clown rather than a sincere Gospel preacher. This behavior has driven out the idea and the possibility of the Church ever being the Church in our lifetime. We are getting worse, instead of getting better. We leave the important leadership in the hands of anyone. I have heard it said among many of our pastors, "When I don't feel like preaching, I let my choir take over." Most choirs in our congregations are made up of clowns. They are taught to be clowns, and they practice to be clowns. Their emotions fly up before the song begins. Most of them have no confession. Most of them have not confessed Christ. Most of them come to the alter for prayer, seeking grace in their lives. That's who you are turning your preaching over to. When did singing or anything else take the place of preaching?

Our preaching is empty. Our style of preaching is not for the Church. Our Church does not preach the kind of preaching that we preach. It is our Church that does the preaching. We'll deal with this later on. Our Church does not tolerate the kind of preaching that we do. Many of us, if we stop sometime and record our message, will find that our Gospel message will last only about five minutes. Our message consists of political humor, sexual commentaries, and other garbage, anything other than the Gospel of Jesus Christ.

We are ignorant to the condition of our people. Look at how many of our ministers will preach sin to the people to help them get rid of sin. You preach more concerning the sins of David than David's salvation. Many people who hear us don't know that David had a life of salvation. All they hear about are his sins, and sin is not to be preached to the Church. The Church doesn't preach sin. Sin is not to be preached to a sinner. Salvation and repentance are to be preached to a sinner. The Gospel of Jesus Christ is to be preached to a sinner. A sinner doesn't need you to preach sin to him; that's what he knows already. He needs to hear the means and sources that are available to help him overcome his sinful state of life.

Ignorance has overtaken us, and we are proud in our ignorance. We exalt our own ignorance. We feel great. We feel proud of our-selves for doing nothing. Most pastors spend their time on the same people, who never change from one year to the next. There's no spiritual growth; there's no spiritual involvement; there's no spiritual lifting; there's no spiritual revival. The only thing people do in our congregations is get old and die.

We lie to them while they live, and when they die, we lie over them after they are gone. This behavior has caused our Church to be criticized, walked on, and be disrespected by the world simply because the Church is not preaching or teaching. And, it's not the Church; it's the individuals, the instruments that we are to be of the Church. We need to wake up. We don't need anyone to tell us that our Church has fallen from grace and fallen to the bottom in the last decade. We don't need anyone to tell us that our Church is cold and boring. Our Church is filled with unsaved people, people who are there to fulfill their intelligence. They came to church Sunday morning because they missed last Sunday morning, and they won't be there next Sunday morning. We have Sunday morning specialists. They go to church on Sunday morning and will not return until the next Sunday morning. We don't believe in evangelism or in soul winning. We believe in social entertainment, musicals, and all kinds of banquets. Everything that the world will allow us to use, we will fantasize in a spiritual manner, use it, and feel good about it. We have failed; we're failing the Church, and the Church is not able to accomplish its mission in the world, simply because we are ignorant about the facts. Many of us have the wrong position because we took it upon ourselves.

The Lord's call is by consent, but many who thought about it went elsewhere and are doing nothing. You cannot expect God to change just because you desire to do something, not because you think it's better, but because you think it's better for you. The Church and the religious world is not a money-making scheme. Churches don't make money; they receive God's money from his people. The Church doesn't angel with government programs and the government mixing in and tying up with the church.

Many have brought the church under the authority of the state and government. This country is based upon the state and the Church being separated.

We draw up charters. Pastors do that. They may legally be bound themselves where they cannot be dismissed by their congregations. If you need the law to keep you as a pastor, you are not one, you never were one, and you'll never be one. God doesn't need the legal system to keep his men where he wants them to be. I think you should look at yourself and see what a fool you're making of yourself in the name of the Kingdom of God.

Do personnel fail the Church? The Church is suffering, meaning the good people are suffering. And the people are seeking a new life in Christ, and they can't find it. Sound doctrine is not being preached and people are not being taught the Word of the Lord. It has been defiled by our selfishness, our styles, and our formalities.

Why don't we move in and get it right or get out. Jesus said, "Don't be like the hypocrites." Hypocrites are standing in the door; they won't come in, and they won't get out of the way to let in someone else. If you are not the man to do, it profits you nothing to live or die, because if you fail, hell will be your home. Hell will be your eternity.

Why do it? Why not repent and clear yourself. It's better to have eternity with Christ than to tamper with him and have eternity in Hell without Christ. It's better to be a laymen with Christ in eternity than to play at being a man of God and go to Hell for eternity. It doesn't make sense.

You do not have to tamper with the Gospel of God or with God's people to make a living. There are other ways. God feeds the fowls of the air. He provides grass for the breast, and, certainly, He provides food for the human beings. Therefore, you certainly don't have to use tricks in order to make it in this world. We are trying to operate our own knowledge and our own self-righteousness, but we had better hurry and submit ourselves unto the righteousness of God. It is God's business. It is God's Church. It is God's will, and it is God's way. We can make it nothing else.

If we are blessed to play a role in it, we are blessed. But to force yourself to be what you're not is a dangerous situation. That's why women are finding out that popularity is to be accomplished. They like popularity. They like pride. They want equal rights with men. They will do anything to be equal to men, not recognizing their ignorance.

There is no way you can be equal to a male when you are a female. You were born a female. You will die a female. You can try to be something else, which puts you out of either one. You are either a male or a female, or you are not either one. You are not counted. God has given you up. You cannot be a man and try to be a woman, or vice versa. You are what God made you and no more.

Many people are talking about they don't know any better, how they are crossed up. We know who we are. We are who we were when we were born, and if you don't understand who you are, look at your birth certificate. Doctors didn't make that kind of mistake. Whoever is on your birth certificate, that's who you are. That's who you were at birth, and that's who you will be when you die. If you want things to be well with you, be the best in being who you are supposed to be.

If you will notice your Bible, ladies, you will find where the leading words or instruction say, he, him, himself, and his, not her, herself, she. You won't find it. Try to refer to what some scriptures sound like, such as taking the first message. You don't know the first message. The prophet carried the first message, the prophet of God, which used such words as pour out my spirit on all flesh. You're right. He did that; He's still doing it. But that's not saying for you to go and preach.

Your life changes in finding the rightful place. Your rightful place is great. You can be no better anywhere than being in place. The best job you can do is the job that you know how to do, and are gifted to do, none other. We, as leaders, better tighten up. Time is beginning to run out on us, and it's not too late to get it right. But when it's too late, it's too late. The prophet summed it up by saying in Isaiah 56:10-11. "His watchmen are blind; they are all ignorant, they are all dumb dogs, they cannot bark; sleeping lying down, loving to slumber. Yea, they are greedy dogs which can never have enough, and they are shepherds that cannot understand: they all look to their own way, everyone to his gain, from his quarter."

Of course, we know that ignorance is made-up of things we don't know about, and if you don't know God, you can't know His will. If you don't know God, you can't know the mission that is to be carried throughout the world. You can't be wise in your calling and ignorant to the works. It doesn't work that way.

The Lord calls everyone who accepts him. He inspires them in their position, according to their ability. He assigns them according to the gifts that He has given them, and He makes a difference between the ministers. He calls the laymen by sending the minister, and he calls the laymen to their responsibility. He calls the minister to his responsibility, and he sends him to cover the others' responsibilities. There is no question, if you know anything about Him, He has called you. But the question is has He sent you? If He didn't send you, then be smart and don't go. He said you are blind to things other than what you are assigned to do. If you are sent, you are blind to the will and works of what He sent you to do.

He will not send you blind, but He will send you wise and well awake so that you might see and be as wise as the Serpent. He says, "They are all ignorant, ignorant to my will, my plans. They are ignorant to what my word is saying. They are ignorant to the word of God. They are ignorant to the plans of God. They are all dumb.

Now, dumb means you can't hear or talk. You can't hear the vision, because it is not sent to you. You can't speak, because you don't know it. God is not going to use you on your free will. He doesn't have to do that. He uses whom he pleases. He doesn't have to substitute anyone. God is not a substituting God. God is the supreme being, and he is self-existence. He doesn't need anyone to do him favors. So, when you're dumb, you can't speak, you can't see wrong. You can't see people doing wrong, and can't tell them. You can't speak, not necessarily that you are physically dumb, that you can't talk at all, but you are dumb to speak where and when you need to speak, because you're not the one to speak. There are always selfish ways to keep you from speaking. You may say, "It's none of my business" You may say, "he or she is not my member" Or, are you going to find some other excuse, when the truth needs to be identified, when lies are being told, and when the truth needs to be represented. The truth needs to be told. When we find our young and old men who misquote the scripture and speak lies in the place of the truth, we should speak, and we will speak if we are not dumb to the situation. So the scripture says, "They are all dumb dogs.'

Now, as you know, when the Bible speaks of dogs, it is referring to a low classification, a low principle, and it bring us in on the level of nothing. They can't bark. They're like a dog that can't bark. A dog cannot earn its place to stay if it cannot bark. A watch dog must be able to bark. It must bark when something is coming near and when the property is being threatened by some stranger, it should be able to bark. If you can't bark when you see something wrong, if you can't speak to correct a wrong, if you can't speak to represent the true righteousness, then you are a dumb dog that cannot bark. Why? Because you love to slumber.

They don't want to become involved. They don't want to be responsible. They love to do nothing. Many pastors try to do as little as they can. They love to slumber and lay around and do nothing. They cannot bark so they sleep. They are greedy dogs.

Many pastors are not interested in the welfare of their people. They want them to be holy, and that's all they care about, not holy enough to do right, but just holy enough to stay with the pastor and do what he asks them to do. Many pastors don't instruct their people, to their best ability, to help them gain progress through life. They will not be too holy to advise their people about who is the best man for office in our government and community. They don't mention that. They don't care if their people have a job as a common laborer or if they are on a fixed income or on welfare. It doesn't matter. They don't think of telling them what steps to take to better their condition.

I think that any pastor should be concerned about the physical welfare of his people. When they give you money, you should think of their sweat, or wonder if they deprived themselves, or wonder how much suffering they have been through. We never think about that. All we want is for them to live up to the bargain and give what is promised to us. We will continue to improve it later on. We are greedy. Our main concern now is our anniversary. We want things that are going to help us on our behalf and we want that to increase. We want a larger salary, and we say it's time to get a raise. Thank God, someone might criticize this, but thank God. I'm a long-time pastor, and I have never discussed a salary or pastored for a salary. I have always been blessed, and I have never had to face the embarrassment of putting a price on my work in preaching the gospel of Jesus Christ. I'm not a greedy person, I'm a thankful person. because I think a little in the name of God is a lot when it gets into my hands. I believe what I preach. I know I have evidence that what he says is real. The word is true; the word of the Lord fulfills itself. All you have to do is trust him.

Also, greedy dogs can never have enough. We trade churches like we trade automobiles. When someone comes up on the auction block with more green, we'll lie about the spirit and say the spirit told us to move and go there. I wonder why the spirit never moves on us to go to a lesser paying or smaller congregation. It always moves us to greater or more We are greedy dogs which can never have enough. The more that we get for ourselves, the more we want, and there are shepherds who can't understand.

You can't understand the will of God: you can't understand his way. If you are only interested in self, and if the shepherd can't understand, what's going to happen to the sheep? The shepherd is the overseer; he's the watchman of the sheep. The shepherd sees after the sheep. He thinks for the sheep. He understands for the sheep because he cares for the sheep's well-being. He feels responsible for the sheep. But you cannot have this kind of responsibility for the sheep within yourself if you are only concerned about yourself. There are shepherds who cannot understand.

You take the place of a shepherd when you are not a shepherd. How then can you understand the needs, the nature of the sheep? How can you train the sheep when you are not a shepherd? How can you know the value of the one sheep that is lost against the ninety-nine that are saved? How can you understand that? How many people have left our congregation and we personally have gone and had a talk with them, picked up the phone and called them, or sent for them to be counseled? How many times? We are only concerned about those who are there. When they leave, they take what they have with them. We no longer have access to their belongings. So go, and we will just wait until next Sunday and somebody else will come.

The fame of my beautiful building is out. The fame of my interior is out. The fame of my singing choir is out. The fame of my preaching and performances is out. So, if someone else is coming, I don't have to worry about losing anyone. Loss does not rest comfortably in the membership of God. This is what all the force is about. this is what the Church about, loss. If it had not been for the loss, there would have not been any church, no need. If it had not been for the loss, Jesus would not have come. If it had not been for the loss, the Lord would not have sent a Church to be born into the hearts of men, because there would have been no need. Who cares about them going somewhere? Others are coming, because my fame is out. It's always me, me, me. It's I who is concerned. It's I who reaped the benefit. It's I who I am concerned about.

They cannot understand. How can you expect people to help you when they don't understand? How can you expect people to proclaim, or to show you life from the Word of God when they do not understand? How can they help you become stronger with your spiritual growth, become stronger in life and in the Lord, when they cannot understand? If you notice, He didn't say they do not understand; He said they cannot understand; That means that they can't. They cannot understand because that is the way they are, and that is the way they are going to be. That's the way they are going to be. If conditions have driven you in this attitude, you have nowhere else to go. If you feel that your pastor, your green pastor is only on this corner, in the middle of this block, you should do what you can to stand by your pastor, because you don't feel that there is another pastor.

God's vineyard has plenty. He has a vineyard wherever He pleases. When He moves from one place, He goes into another, because God has pastors who no one has taken anything out of. They are very green. They cannot understand that they all look to their own way. Everyone is for his own gain. You don't trust God for your way. You don't trust your ministry or God's will in your life. You say God gave you five senses, and you're supposed to take them over and use them. You are only looking to your way. Your way is different from God's.

"My ways are above man's way, as high as the heavens of the earth," says the Lord. Man's way has never been the way of the Lord. The Lord said, "I am the way, and in the way that I am, all your needs are in the way." All of your life, what you need and where you are going is in the way of the Lord, not your way. Everyone, goes his way everyone, for his gain, from his quarter. If we think about what we are going to accomplish and gain, then how, for Pete's sake, are we going to expect eternal life? Who would settle for a world of things instead of a life of eternity? Who would give up the opportunity of eternity with Christ? That we might build treasures and have these kinds of luxuries in this life? What does it profit a man to gain the whole world and lose his own soul?

The only thing that a man has in this world to call his own, and that the Scripture has called his, is his soul and his sins. These are yours, your sins. See God get rid of them. Your soul, give it to the Lord, and He will save your soul. Your soul is the only part about you that will not die. Your soul is going to live forever somewhere. Your sins are going to burn with your soul if you don't find forgiveness. It's your soul, not you, but your soul. You have the option. You can save your soul, or you can continue as you are and lose it and spend eternal life in eternal hell fire. That's all you have.

You claim a lot of things. You claim land, houses, authority, and businesses. You claim all of these things, but you are only using these things; they are being lent to you. The only thing you have access to call your own is your soul and your sins. When you commit sins, they become your sins. You didn't make up that sin. You left and took on that sin. You found the sins in the world. Whatever sin you commit, remember that many people have committed that same sin long before you got there. That's why the Scripture teaches us. "Yield not unto temptations." Sin is there; stay away from it. Don't become a part of it. But first you have to get rid of that in you through total repentance. We repent and get rid of who we are, sinners. We then become an opposition. We become lives without sin, and we have to stay away from it. We can accept it. We can lean towards it and accept it, or we can reject it, and feel free from it. That's what your Scriptures teach, and that's what the book of Romans teaches, and it is true.

Sin doesn't look for you. It's there, and you become involved in it in your daily life. We have to be aware of the enemies that we have in this world, and sin is one of them. Sin and Satan are so combined they breathe and live together. They are as one. As the Spirit of God and his Word are one, sin and Satan are one.

Let us remember that sin is always around, and Satan will maneuver. Satan is the author. Satan is the flesh, and the spirit sin is the breath of him. They are one. When you learn to stay free from , you are also free from his sin. But to deal with Satan, to live with him and to work with him, you are working in his sinful stage.

Many of us who say we can't help ourselves don't believe that. We believe that sin is to be committed. But you don't have to commit sin. It is a choice that you make. Always where there is a wrong, right is present. Always where there is bad, good is present. It is always the option there. It's up to us to choose which one we want to make. Many teach that you can't help it; you just wake up and breathe. Yes, if you have never been saved, you breathe sins. When you accept Christ, that saves you, because Christ has saved already. You have been saved already. That's not preached, but it is true. Christ has saved, and the only thing people have to do is accept. When you accept Christ in your life, he saves you. By coming in your life, he saves you, because he has saved already. He has suffered and paid the price already. He has already gained the victory, and the only thing for us to do is receive Him and believe that He has given us freedom, given us eternal life, and given us the cause to confess, to live for Him and to seek His way.

Anyone who accepts Christ submits himself unto Him. Anyone who accepts Christ doesn't just get Christ by His lips or His words. You can't accept Christ that way. Your lips confess only what the heart has done. If you accept Him with all of your heart, then your mouth will tell what the heart has done. When that happens, it means that you have accepted Christ in your life. There must also be evidence. Accepting Christ is demonstrating in the new life that you have made in this transition. The change has taken place, and that's what we will never forget. That's a memory, because nothing else can make such an impact in our lives. It is being changed; it is being born. Nothing else is like being born. Life does not begin until you are born.

We have a problem, and man comes and confuses the issue, and the time, the impact that he places upon these things. It blinds us when we come to life. One situation that has confused, and blocked the heart of many people concerning themselves is the confused state of emotion. When you really look into it, it is a guessing game. One side of a crowd says one thing, and the other says another. Instead of sitting down, working it out, and coming to a common ground, the human family hasn't learned how to do that. We find ourselves making wrong worse and moving right further away.

One thing that every man should understand is that you can't be right and wrong at the same time. You are right or wrong. Everybody can't be right or wrong at the same time. Where there is right, there is wrong, and the most important thing is having to decide to want to be right and knowing that you are right. Anytime that you have to force your right, right doesn't need to be forced. Right just needs a little time. The whole world knows where right stands, so anytime you have to force people to be right, something is wrong, because you can't make right be right. Right is right without your assistance or without your forcing it to be right. It's an emotion that has touched the lives of the entire nation.

People have blown it out of proportion. It has exhaulted and incited their anger, and they have tried to force their rights. They have tried to take action upon what they think is wrong. Doctors and other people have lost their lives, because other people say they are right and want to force their rights.

They say they love the unborn soul. They say they will die for the unborn, but how much are they doing for the ones who have been born? How can you love the unborn better than you love those who have been born? Why do you want to die for the unborn, and you don't want to feed the born? We can come up with some of the most terrible ideas, and we can do some strange things. In the midst of all that, the Bible says, "Life begins when you are born." That's what the Bible says; you become a human being when you are born. Now at the thought of life, life itself is in the framework of God. If God's word says that life begins when you are born, what difference does it make about what we say, because we are not bringing about life. We are not bringing forth human lives. Do we really know any other way? Are you saying that the Lord doesn't have it right, or the Lord is not telling the truth? I don't think so.

I believe that we should think about what we are doing and what we're talking about and stay in the framework of man's ability and man's responsibilities. Man's law doesn't go beyond the birth of this world. When we're born into this world, we're born to the law of the land, and when we die, we go out of the law of the land. To make laws on something that we have never been in is kind of ridiculous, but so what? We do a lot of things that are ridiculous.

But the truth and sound doctrine about the word of God needs to be preached, uncompromised, and with courage and sincerity of heart, from man's dedication according to what he has been commissioned to do. When we can't find very much for which to live and nothing for which to die, I guess life doesn't mean very much. When the Christian life isn't there, the Christian growth is not there. In what other way can eternity be pointed out other than through the life of Christianity and the word of God. These lives become so useless, because they are so low in value. It's a disaster when our churches fail, and don't come up to their full responsibility.

Life is promised from God, I mean eternally, because life is given by God. God is the life of every life. Man has no dominion over life. That's why it is hard to understand how man can take a life legally. How can it be legal to take a life? Can the legal system give a life? I don't think so. No one should take what they cannot give.

We have a lot of problems in every step of life simply because of the failure of the three institutions in life. When we leave home a failure, we are going to be a failure in school and a failure in church. There's room for repentance. We can repent and overcome some of these things. But if you haven't repented the first time, then you don't know anything concerning repentance.

If you notice our Christian testimony is empty. It has no inspiration and nothing to attract others to seek it. It demonstrates no change, and being born means the beginning. Accepting Christ is being born. When you accept Christ, that means a new life begins. Life only begins with Christ. With Christ out of your life, there's no life to count. With Christ out of your life, out of your home, and out of your community, there's a dangerous atmosphere. Christ is all. The Spirit of God is available through the Church to penetrate our community and to demonstrate God is with us He is present and His hand is reaching to those who know Him not.

Now ministers, if we don't convert our people into understanding who they are, then it's hard to explain their responsibility. Your responsibility depends upon who you are. If you don't know who you are, then how will you know what your responsibilities are. If you don't know that you are the Church, the Church by the new birth, how will the Church is to live and function through you? It's sad. It's sad that we have settled with an organization. We have built an organization within our people, and they have functioned within the regulation of the organization. They have believed in their organization.

They have treated the organization as if it belongs to them. They have no fear of God. They have no respect for the man of God. They have no confidence in the man of God, and they don't have the patience or reason to believe in what He says. In the first place, if you speak of Christ, they don't know who you're talking about. They are known to be our outstanding people and representatives the Church, but they haven't been born of the Spirit of God.

If you haven't been born, you cannot be the Church. The Church is born into the hearts of men and women. The Church is alive The Church is life. It's the life of Christ. It comes only through the second birth.

Baptism is not essential for salvation. It is not intended to save but to give the evidence that you have confessed that you are saved. We need to become more sound in our teaching and dedicate our lives to teaching sound doctrine. Any doctrine taught by the Lord Jesus Christ, and the doctrine of the Church as it was introduced by the Apostle, will prepare people with an evangelistic attitude toward each other. The only way that we can accomplish our mission is through us to others, by us, and to reach others and lead them to Christ.

We can perform only according to our ability. We can act only according to our inner portion. If Christ is the new man, and the new creator in us, then we are a new creature. We're not excited about old things, because they have passed, and all things became new by Him. Life is new. Our outlook is new. We have a testimony, we have a new desire, a new outreach, and a certainty about our responsibility to others. It will become known that we will be able to carry out the assignment for every believer to conduct himself correctly and to make a spiritual accomplishment in the world in which we live. Isn't it something that we see the world around us is suffering because of the lack of something we were supposed to have and should have rendered unto them? It should make us feel kind of responsible for the world around us, because if we had the opportunity to meet them in their loss, help them in their emptiness, and bring good news to them that would change their lives, yes it is our responsibility. We can start. We won't be able to accomplish anything until we start in the right direction.

So, time is on a countdown. Only what we do for Christ will stand in the judgment. Only what we do for Christ will make us obtain our eternal purpose. The Lord knows. He knows all about us. He knows all of our failures and faults, and He knows all the efforts. He knows that the failures are our own inner ability. He knows it all.

I think we should understand that there's nowhere to hide. How shall we escape if we neglect so much of salvation?

The question is, what is the Church? What is this great, divine spiritual institution? What is it? Is it a house that's built on the corner? No. Is it a house that is built in the middle of the block or on the side of the road? No. Is it a house that is built with a steeple on top? No. What are those houses? They are the houses of God and not the Church. Out of all of our teaching and preaching, isn't it sad that our people don't know the difference between the house of God and the Church? They believe that the Church is the house of God. Some have great testimonies. We preach to them, but we do not explain to them that the house of God is not the Church. God had his house long before the New Testament Church was born. But when God built the Church, He didn't build the Church out of a house.

Now, let me ask you a question. If the home is not a part of the Church, or if the home is not the Church, then what happens to the Church when they leave the house of God and go home? See how many answers you will get. The house of God is required. God requires us to build him a house. The disciples thought that when Jesus ascended He was going to build a house and a Church. They asked Him the question when He was getting ready to ascend, "When will you restore the kingdom back to Israel?" His answer was, "That it is not meant for you to know; that is in my father's providence." When the time comes, He will answer that. The house, what we have, and the place of the Church is an organization, and we have our own plans to operate it.

"If Jesus had built the Church in a house, it would have been destroyed. There is no way it would have survived two thousand years and still been living and real. How in the name of Pete's sake can the Church be a house and survive? You can hardly keep the Lord's house built now, and it's supposed to be a civilized country. People have nothing else to do but burn it down. They think that they are burning the Church, but they are not burning the Church. They are burning God's house. There is no way that they can burn the Church, and that was the purpose of the Lord building His Church into the hearts of men, so it will live until the mission is over. The Church that Christ built had to be a living church, a preaching church, a teaching church, a witnessing church, a shouting church, and a church that is a soul-winning church. The Church is making poor progress, because most of our people don't know what it is.

Most ministers think that the church is theirs, that the Church is the cross that they wear on their neck or that the Church is some kind of sign on an automobile. The Church is everyone who confesses Christ. We have completely dehumanized the Church and God until we know so little about either one of them.

The actual New Testament Church is spread throughout the world. It had to be for the multiplying of the people. There are many congregations There are many assemblies, but there is one Church. We preach to people and teach them that when you come to Jesus, or come to Christ, He is in some kind of business or works. Every time that someone comes and gives the preacher his hand, the Lord comes and saves him. Not so, the Lord has saved the world. He saved them all at the same time. He came one time. He suffered one time. He died one time, and He rose one time. He died for us instead; He rose for our justification, and He saved all. All that an individual would have to do is accept Him, accept Him as Savior and as Lord. When they accept Him, and He receives them, they are saved. They are born again, and they become new creatures in Him. When you receive Him, you receive the Church. The Church is His, and the Church comes through him. Even when the Church was born through the power of the Holy Ghost on the day of Pentecost, the Church, and the Holy Ghost came in the same package. The Holy Ghost came in power, and the Church came testifying. When you receive Christ, you receive the Church. The Church comes to us in the form of an organization that we were meant to use as a system of getting our people in fellowship and working together. We have completely taken that. Instead of them working together, we preach to them that this is the Church, and this is all of it. That is our mistake. The Church, when you accept Christ, meaning when you receive the Holy Spirit or the Holy Ghost (whichever way you pronounce it, it means the same thing), you receive the Church, and you become one of the saints of God. You are converted from a sinner to a saint.

Now, some of our leaders have said through the ages that we have become saved sinners, and that's not even a divine terminology. That's just an ignorant remark. (It does not show people who they were, and they will never know as long as they believe that they are a saved sinner.) Do you think that the Lord can save your life without changing you? Anyone's life is who has accepted Christ. They have sense enough to know that they are not a sinner; they are not the same. They are not capable of being the same. They do not consist of being the same. So, you are the Church, and you are ready to perform in the Church or as the Church, not just on Sunday mornings, not just when you go to the house of God, but even in your house or wherever you go. It changes your lifestyle. It changes your personality. It changes your dealings. You deal rightly and righteously. You have a different outlook on life, because it is a new life. You love instead of hate. You help instead of hurt. You are righteous instead of unrighteous. You are a changed person, because you are the Church. You have been inserted into the position that the Lord has for you to function in the Church. (The difference in the organization that you know about you are in it; that's why we say that we belong to the Church.) We belong to Antioch. We belong to Mt. Moriah. We belong to Mt. Olive, and that is what our heart allows. That's what we believe in and that's it. Mt. Moriah or Mt. Olive is not the name of your Church; it's the name of your location. It's the name of your title or location, but your church is named the Church. Those long before us said that the Church is the group of the called out, baptized and believers. That's a little too casual. The Church is a group of born-again believers.

Now, if you are talking about the second baptism, then that might work, but for this group of born again believers, you can be the Church through birth only, not through water baptism, because water baptism does not save you. Water baptism was never designed to save. Water baptism is a fulfillment from the Levitical rules of the Church. Water baptism is a mark of obedience; it's a sign and the fulfillment of circumcision.

Circumcision was known to be the religious sex of the Church. The circumcision could not fit in the New Testament Church, because if it had, woman would have been excluded from the Church. Water baptism is the marking sign, and you only take on water baptism after you have been saved by the power of the Holy Spirit and not before. The Church was born. The Church was born on the day of Pentecost, and we are born of Christ when we accept Him, and the Church is established in our hearts. When we have accepted Christ and the Church is established in our hearts, we begin a mission in our lives, which the Church performs in our lives. The Church carries out the mission. The Church is the mission. The church is established in the hearts of men so that man cannot destroy the Church. It's the living Church. It's the church none other than the New Testament Church. These name-calling organizations that try to convince us that we are in the Church when we are at the house of God and that we will leave the Church at the house of God and have no Church at all are ridiculous. If the Church is not in our home, then how can we assemble in the house of the Lord for worship service. The use of the house of God is for the Church to move in, to come in and worship, and go out and serve. We serve God each day, everyday. We worship the Lord when we come together and congregate at the house of God. The life of the Church is our new life and commitment to salvation.

The Church keeps, directs, and leads us to all steps of life. We live together. We work together. We represent the Church wherever we go. Your church can be no more than you. Whatever you are and however you present yourself, however you conduct your life, is your church.

If our homes cannot measure up to our church at the house of God, then we are really not that church. We are really not born again people. The Church at home is our keeping power.

If your lifestyle doesn't measure up to your church at the house of God, then you are not the Church at either place. It's impossible for you to be the Church at the house of God and be something else at your house. The Church is needed more at your house than it is at the house of God, because you must be the Church to worship the Lord in spirit and in truth at the house of God. You must be the Church to live a righteous life in your own home. In other words, if something is at your home that the Church will not accept, you either remove that from your home, or the Church will be moved from your life. It's just as simple as that. How can we live for Christ and we have no church to live in us? Paul said, "It's not I that liveth, but He that liveth in me."

It is impossible to please God in the flesh. It is impossible to carry out the principles and the requirements of our brotherhood and fellowship between one and another without the life from the inside, which is the Church. The Church is keeping directing, and teaching us with the keeping power to manage together, to live together, and to get along with each other.

If we were the Church, our community would be better. If we were the Church and the Church were in the homes, the communities would be better, because the children would be better. The lack of the Church in our homes is the destruction of our land today. You will never be able to have the kind of community that human beings should live in, in peace and unity, until the Church takes control in our homes. We will never be able to see each other as brothers and sisters, regardless of who or where, until the Church is in our hearts, so that it can dwell in our homes.

You need the Church more at home than any other place. It is where you live. You feel freer to do wrong at home than at any other place. I have heard many people who have spoken out and said that they will settle their arguments and disputes when they get home. The language is different at home. Everything is different at home. If you are able to live a righteous life at home without the Church, then that means that you can live it anywhere without the Church.

So, it is important to understand that God will not require us to do something that we cannot do. He has provided the way. It's not God's mistake that we fail to learn, that we fail to accept Christ, and that we fail to stay at His foot until we learn His way and His will. Jesus said, "If any man comes after me, let him deny himself, take up the cross, and follow me." He didn't say follow me to the house of God. He didn't say follow me on highways or dangerous byways of life. He said, "Follow me." That means daily; that means every step. Follow Him. And when He established the Church in us, He planted life in us that we might be able to not only follow Him, but to reach out to others to join in and follow Him.

We cannot be the Church, we cannot reap the blessings of the Church until we learn what it is. You know if Jesus had been going to our schools, two thousand years later we would still have Him in elementary school.

Jesus came to the world, because God made Him for the betterment and for redemption on Earth. His son gave His life, took our place in death, died instead of us, and rose to our justification. We are still calling on Him as the son of God. He said Himself after His resurrection that, "All power has been given to me in Heaven and Earth." Peter said in Acts 2:36, "Therefore let all the house of Israel know assuredly, that God hath made the same Jesus, whom ye have crucified, both Lord and Christ." He is Lord in our lives. The son God made was not a heavenly mission; it was an earthly mission. The son of God did not come from Heaven. The son was born on Earth. The son lived on earth, the son suffered on earth, the son died on earth. He died on earth and separated Himself from the earthly birth. The son was buried, and Jesus Christ rose. The son died, and Jesus Christ rose. In other words, He who was born on Earth, died on

Earth, and that which took on the body on Earth rose. He is Lord, not just your savior because He is saved. He saved all. He saved every creature at one death, at one suffering, at one resurrection. The only thing that is left for us to do is receive, and we receive it when we accept Him in our hearts and lives. So with everything that Jesus took on, including His name, His name did not come from Heaven; His name is an earthly name. The name Jesus was given by the prophets. He took on that name on His earthly mission, and when his earthly mission was finished, He departed, and left the name that we live by. It is the only name between the Heaven and the earth, whereby men can be saved. In order to pray to God, we must pray by that name. We must live by that name. We must do all things by the name of Jesus. That will be easy to understand if people will stop trying to dehumanize God, and will try to understand His word and study more archeology of the Bible so that we can understand the time, place, purpose, and actions. We will be able to teach the contents of the cross, to preach the proper contents of the cross. Many of us don't know the contents of what we are preaching when we are dealing with or thinking of the cross. The question is, are you preaching to the cross, are you preaching from the cross, or are you preaching in the cross? It is very important to know, because you cannot confess them. Every direction and every time and period must be in its own proper perspective.

Jesus taught and preached on Earth. He taught from the prophets. He taught concerning the establishment of salvation. He talked about his Kingdom. Many things He talked about. He talked to people about the condition of the human family at the actual time He was on Earth. We take the things that he taught others about and try to apply them exactly with today's life. All things will not work. It's a message from God. God's Word is a living word. It has today's message to every individual who rises in the morning. It has today's message, and the message is direct from God, because it's from the word of God. It is direct to the individual, and it will meet their needs of the present time. Many times we say the Gospel is a story. The Gospel of Jesus Christ is not a story. History is a story. The Gospel of Jesus Christ is the living Word of God. History is something that has been experienced already; it has been written already, and nothing changes. The Gospel of Jesus Christ cannot be totally explained; it's the living Word. The more you preach the more is there. The deeper you study, the more it is there. There is no way to measure the dimensions of God's Word. When you think of the dimension of it, it is wider than the width, it is higher than the heights, it is deeper than the depths. There is no way to sum it up or to gather it up as a total. It is a living Word, and God is beyond measurement. God is bigger than the world he made.

God fills up the world. Many times in our prayers, we tell the Lord to come over here, or stop by here, or guard here, but God does not come or go. He filled his world. He built his world. He is bigger than the world He built. That is because He fills up His world and fills up the outside of His world, because He is holding the world that He made in His own hands. So, He is there. He is everywhere. He covers every inch of space that can be discovered by any man. When we gather our stories and rhymes and our so-called messages to preach to the people, I think that we should seek and be the messenger of God. If you don't receive the message from God, it's not worth being preached. If you don't receive the word by the revelation and inspiration of God, then it is not the Gospel of Jesus Christ, the only one. The only one, the Gospel of Jesus Christ. Paul said, "If any, even the angels preach any other Gospel, let them be of a curse." He's the only source of salvation and the only remedy for men to be saved by the name of Jesus Christ. It is important, pastors, for us to stop kidding ourselves, to stop fantasizing about our ministry and get down to the truth and the sound doctrine, and to let our people know the difference between the Church, the church house, the house of God, and the Church of the living God. When we get this in order, then we can convert people enough to make the corrections in the other institutions and bring the world into some order, if it is to happen before Jesus calls the order.

I think that we need to do all that we can, while we can, to overcome some of these blunders and failures that we have made through lives and generations. Do not let salvation be as a joke in the minds of people, because it is not a joke. It is real. It is what it means and that is deliverance, deliver once from one state of life unto another, and it does not supply round trips. When you are delivered from the state of a sinful life unto Christ and you feel what the Holy Spirit has become in that Church, it fills your life. That is the only way that we can be children of God and servants of God. We have to be filled with all of Him. He has to work in all of us, and the Church fills our lives. It fills our days. It fills our months. It becomes the way of life. It drives out these kinds of sinful acts: hatred, envy, and strife, and all of the things that have corrupted our communities and our governments throughout the land, simply because it has been provided for us to be the kind of people who make the right communities, the right homes, the right churches, and the right governments. It is not being used now, because it is misunderstood. It is the purpose of being able to determine what it is like. It is to repent, to totally surrender unto the Lord, to take on the whole armor, and to let Him make us what He would, and that is the Church of the living God. When this takes place, there will be no problem living a righteous life. The Church is righteous. I've heard many people say, I've heard radio people say there is no such thing as a perfect church. Maybe they have not been made aware of the day of Pentecost. Maybe they are not aware that it was Jesus Christ Himself who came in the power of the Holy Ghost. Maybe they were not aware that the Church was born through this power.

Just think of the wonderful excitement that went on in that small period of time in the upper room when the power came down.

The power came as a rushing wind. When the Church came in and lit upon those who waited, they began to speak as God gave them utterance.

The world has not been the same, as far as the Church is concerned. Isn't it sad that so many of us have yet to get the message? We have yet to find ourselves in this New Testament Church? We have yet to find ourselves filled with the glory and happiness of his Church that was born in the hearts. Won't it be wonderful when men can begin to testify of this Church working in them and reach out for the lost and have compassion for the poor, as well as live together in peace and unity. That's the Church. The Church does not consist of violence. The Church does not create violence. The Church does not create hate. The Church does not preach hate. The Church does not preach envy, The Church does not preach separation or some up and some down. The Church does not look on the human family in a color-blind situation. The Church is the Kingdom of our Lord that is living and functioning in the lives of those who have accepted and who are caught up in doing the will of God. The Church is not an organization that is operated by unconverted people. Throughout our congregations and our organizations, our organizations fall short on prayer services, short on testimonies, and short on demonstrating brotherhood and fellowship through the community. They are lifted in pride. It's a race with the world; it floods the stadium. The world is interrupted by the people of the Church routing them out of their place. The world cannot enjoy their portion of the world and their good times because of the presence of the people out of the so-called Church. But that is not the church; that is not the works of the Church.

The Church is a spiritual operation, not something to have you all out of control at all times. The Church is there on your jobs on the roads you travel, and wherever you go. It teaches when you need to be taught. It keeps you when you need to be kept. It controls you when you need to be controlled. It gives you the power to hold your peace when it's not time to speak. It gives you the truth to speak the truth when it needs to be spoken. It serves every purpose for every time and place. It's there. It's intelligent. It's not moveable. It's unchangeable. It's in you and working everyday. It controls your hands and minds. It controls your feet. It is all about you, and it keeps you in control at all times. This is what the Church is all about. It's a life, a living life, a spiritual life, a righteous life. This is of what the Church consist. The church is not to be controlled by unconverted people. because this Church will not end up in the heart of unconverted people. It's only established in you when you accept Christ and are filled with the Holy Spirit. That brings about a change in your life. You are not the old Adam, but you become the new Adam of Christ.

Let us think about all of these years. In all of these hundreds of years that have gone by, we know so little. We have so little experience, because we never recognize the three institutions that make up our lives. These three institutions hold the general principles of God's will and way. Check it out. Find out that what exists on the outside of the home, school, and Church, God will not ordain it. God will not accept it. God will not receive it when He comes. Of Jesus, Paul says many times, "He will appear." Now this is more understandable in line with Jesus's coming, because when we say He's coming after the Church, then it moves us to speculate some idea that Jesus will come from somewhere and that He will appear in some form and come from Heaven or somewhere. Jesus has come already. He returned ten days after his ascension. The only time that Jesus was absent from the earth since He came as the Son of God was when He returned to Heaven as Lord and was visible to the world and returned back as invisible in power in the Church. And He hasn't left since. When will He appear? He doesn't have to come back, He's here. But when will He appear from the invisible to the visible and to call to order His own world? When He comes and captures His own Church, when he calls his own Church to a halt, those who are sleeping in Him and those who are living in Him will have special consideration, because He promised to come and to receive the Church that He built, the Church that He built through birth on the day of Pentecost, the Church to which He gave the New Covenant, and the Church to which He called his disciples and made them apostles. He also inspired them to write His Word and to institute His doctrine concerning Him and His Kingdom. When all of the things shall come and time shall bring the last moment around, Jesus will appear and call His world to order. As of now, we're still at work, still preparing for this moment to come. We are this Church. We are in this Church. We are preaching and telling men to call.

Many times we give instructions to those who we are trying to teach. We tell them to ask God to forgive them for all of their sins. I don't think that's firm enough to tell them. Tell them to ask God to forgive them for what they are and to forgive them as a sinner. Until He forgives them as a sinner and changes them from a sinner to a saint, forgiving them for all of their sins is not going to serve the purpose, because if you are a sinner, you are a sin-maker. If He forgives you for all your sins, in a matter of hours, you are surrounded in sin again, because no man can please God in the flesh until Jesus comes into your life and takes control of the inner man so that you can and live the righteous life and live according to His Word. Jesus Himself is the author and finisher of our faith. We will have to make sure that we have surrendered and given ourselves to Him and He has established His Church and His Kingdom in us so that we can work until it is complete. For the building of His Kingdom, Jesus did not allow us to go out and carry on with our general principle or what we can pick up or learn from each other or some kind of way to confuse the truth. No. He didn't do that. He went away. When Jesus went away, He was with man. He was with His disciples. They were with Him. And when they were with Him, they were sinners like everyone else, and they remained that way until He went away and came back. He went away with us; He came back in us. In, in, in. In the second chapter of Acts, that little word "in" is mentioned twenty five-times—in us, the Holy Spirit in us, the Church in us, in them, he comes in. He filled them. In, in. We are in Christ; Christ is in us. We were born of Him. We were born of the Spirit of God, which means that we are in Christ, and when we were born in Him, He then established the Church in us. We became the temple for the Church, because when we accepted Him, and we were in Christ, He established the Church in us.

So, we are in Christ, and the Church is in us. The Church is His. He is the head of the Church. His Spirit is the life of the Church that works in us. I think that you should understand this. You might disagree, but check it out. Check it out spiritually, and if you don't have anything better, believe it, and trust it, and trust it because this is it. This is sound doctrine. This is the sound truth of the Church. It is in your Bible. It is to be preached by you. So, you are going to have to accept this in order to be able to preach.

If you are preaching, it's either the truth or a lie. That is left for you to judge. You cannot be right and wrong at the same time. If you are not preaching the truth, you are preaching a lie, and preaching doesn't need anything but the Word of God, only the Word. Only the Word is going to save mankind. Only the Word is going to prepare us to be suitable and able to serve that Church.

When we accept Jesus, He receives us; we find ourselves in Jesus. Then He establishes the Church in us. Remember when the Church was born, it was born in a house, but it didn't stay in the house very long, because it outgrew the house. No house has been able to hold the Church since. Many houses have been built, but no house can hold the New Testament Church. It can hold congregations, and all congregations must be under the railing of the New Testament Church. You can call yourself whatever you want. You can name your titles. You can name your church. You can name it St. Paul, Mt. Olive, New York, Antioch, or whatever you want to name it, but the Church is the Church. You can name it a black church or a white church or whatever you want to name it, but it must practice the teaching of Jesus Christ, the Apostles' doctrines. It must practice redemption. It must promote the New Testament Church and the building of the Kingdom of our Lord. You cannot split this Church with colors or creeds. You cannot make one group right and the other one wrong.

You must be the New Testament Church, and if you are the New Testament Church, we should understand each other. It shouldn't be any problem for us to communicate. It shouldn't be any problem to respect, honor, and appreciate each other. If we are of the New Testament Church, there is no doubt about us getting along. We will love each other. We will walk together. We will live in the same world in peace and harmony. We will go to school together. We will worship together. We will enjoy each other. We will share each other's burdens. These are the functions of the New Testament Church.

Any person who preaches hate is not of Jesus Christ. Any person who preaches of bitterness and confusion and any person who boosts the rich and squashes the poor is not of Jesus Christ. The Church is a Church of the living God, which brings people together in one fellowship, one faith, one Lord, and one baptism. There is only one judgment, and there is only one roundup. When Jesus comes, many people say that they are going to Heaven, but we don't know about that. We do not have any records that say we are going to Heaven. We are told that Jesus said that He is coming back to receive us unto himself. We are not to preach after His coming; we are to preach His coming. When He comes, preaching is over. When he comes, no man knows what will take place. You can put Scriptures together, and that's our problem. We try to fit Bibles, books, and Scriptures, and we take Scriptures that are not even related to each other to prove our points and to make good stories and good speeches, but that doesn't make it sound. We preach the coming of Christ, and when Christ comes He doesn't need us to do anything, because He will call the order. And it is not a labored situation, because God speaks from His mouth. He creates from His mouth. He fights with His mouth; He heals with His mouth. Therefore, He doesn't need anyone else. He just speaks the word.

Many people use the saying, because they picked it up from someone else that when they die they are going to Heaven. Can you imagine that? The Lord didn't tell us to go to Heaven; He told us to go to worship. He told us to go and labor in his vineyard. He said that he would come and receive us. He will save us the problem and journey to go anywhere. He is coming, and when he is there, we may be also.

So, not only have we lost touch and lost the way, we have lost the message. We have forgotten what we are preaching, and for whom we are preaching.

It seems that we are preaching for reputation or to be glorified by those who hear us. The only excitement that we can really enjoy is from those who become victims of the Gospel, turn from their wicked ways, and come to accept Christ in their lives—accept Christ and be in Christ so that the Church can be in them and they can be able to labor and work out their souls' salvation.

Your works are to be within the Church. Many people say they don't need a church. Well, you don't need a church, you need the Church. All of those churches houses that you have around and that you're calling churches, you're right, we don't need them. You only need one Church, and that is the New Testament Church, the only Church that was built in the hearts of men. We build these huge buildings, with thousands of dollars, and millions of dollars, and we back up and say, "That's our church." I remember when Jesus looked at buildings because of the minds of those who were following Him. He said, "There will not be a stone left in turn, but I will raise up a building in three days that will not be destroyed." So, He did that. He rose. He rose on the third day, and within the fifty days, He had built the Church in the hearts of that one hundred and twenty men and women who waited by His instruction until they received power. Some of the disciples who experienced Him breathing on them, received the Holy Ghost, but they didn't receive power until they assembled and waited in Jerusalem. After the Church was filled with the power of the Holy Spirit, they had to come down out of the upper room, and it filled the city. And in this time, they were celebrating and praising God, and Peter preached Jesus. The number of people grew from one hundred and twenty to around three thousand.

We have no record about whether policemen showed up. Where were the policemen? There wasn't anyone but men praising God and some screaming and saying what must we do to be saved. They were filled with the Church. They were in Jesus, and the Church was in them multiplying.

Somewhere, since then, we changed questions. Somewhere we landed in huge buildings and houses and made up our own doctrines, set our own standards of living, painted our own pictures, and made our own Gods. We set our own rules and regulations, and we have been driven away from the Spirit of the New Testament Church. Our community, our schools, our churches, and our governments are suffering from it today. They are suffering because the churches are not producing the kind of men and women that the community needs.

It is said today that your television screen is filled with men who are supposed to be intelligent, government men, even from our capital, and they talk and act like wild people. They act like tigers that are ready to claw each other to pieces. They don't act like men who are intelligent or like men who are representing the great country, and a peaceful community. If those kinds of people are sent Washington to perform and to conduct themselves like mad people, are you saying that they are your best people? Let's make sure we don't send the worst people there, because they demonstrate bad examples. I wonder, do they think if they don't do a better job with their works than their attitude, they have failed already? It's not only the men of the government. We as ministers, don't conduct ourselves like men of God. We act more like sports figures, gangsters, and playboys, with our diamonds and jewelry and long fingernails, which is sad. It's a disgrace the type of personality we expose to the world. It's a long way from appearing as a man of God.

The Scripture says, "Let your light so shine before men that they may see your good works." It is our responsibility to be what we are and represent ourselves as being our natural selves If you don't stand for something, you will fall for anything.

We must think of who we are representing and our expectations of our help. Depend on God's revelations. Exhault God through his Spirit, and humble yourselves while doing so. You don't have to make displays or commercialize your office. Just fill it. When you fill your office, it will speak for itself. When you bring the messages from God to the people, they will know that you have been with Jesus.

I think that we should be disgusted to see people react and see them conduct themselves as if we have not preached. We see everything except what we preach. I know that many people have wondered and thought about why the people we pastor don't even practice what we preach. They are caught up. They set their own standards. They make their own moves. They present themselves. But we see nothing of the results of what we preach. Now, it's either that the people are not saved or we are not preaching what we think we are preaching. Something is not working, and I think that it is our responsibility to make an inventory to evaluate what we are preaching. We should record our messages; listen to them. If something is off target, and if we preach a sound doctrine, stand up for what we preach. It will make a difference.

Therefore, this is evidence that we, as pastors and ministers, have failed. The home has failed. The school has failed. The preachers and the churches have failed. No one can correct this failure alone. The government can't do it. The school alone cannot do it. The home cannot do it. We must be in unity. Ministers must spend more time at the schools. The school needs you to be present; they need your counseling. They need you to come and give some time at the school to establish this relationship between the school and the home. Until this happens, we will not make a start at correcting this great falling away from this great break-away that took place even before we came into the scene, but we have to start somewhere. We might not be able to fulfill everything about it, but we can make an attempt. If we make a start, those who will follow us may succeed. A restorative relationship between the home, school, and church is the only way that men and women can become the kind of men and women who deserve the kind of country they live in, the kind of home they are able to live in, the kind of schools they have an opportunity to attend, and the kind of church that has remained available. We need to change and bring our relationship back together and get in harmony with God, or we will lose it all. It's just as simple as that. It would be a disaster, and, remember, God gives it to us, and He can take it away. It is His. He just lets us use these things, and He can take them whenever he pleases. But by obedience, He will bless us more together. God does not bless the divided. Divided people, divided homes, and a divided kingdom cannot stand. Togetherness, where there is unity, there is strength. Where there is togetherness, God blesses.

So, other ministers, we have a chance to restore a lot of what has been undone. We hold the possibility of improvement and overcoming. We must take the lead in this situation. We must take the lead, because we are the ones to warn the people and call their attention to the condition that we are in, the dangers we are facing, and the disasters into which we are headed. If we don't do it, then who will? If not now, when? We trust that this alarm will go off in all four corners of the globe, and we are causing men to think, to come to their senses, and to remember that God is not pleased. It is a matter of time before He will call us to judgment. He will call us in, and declare the time will be no more It will be too late then. We have a chance now. We have a chance to do something about all of what is undone, all for which we are responsible, all that has failure pointing in our direction.

Preaching is God's purpose of saving mankind. When we fail to preach, when we fail to teach, and when we fail to sound the warnings, a man's life and destruction is required to our hands. That is planned by God. We cannot force or make them do anything, but we can warn them. We can sign the law that they might change. Some will change. Some will take heed, because many of our people know that something is wrong, but they are unable to put their finger on it. They are unable to determine what it is, but we, as men of God, hold the problem. We know where the failure lies, but many of us want to turn the deaf ear and blame it on somebody else, but it just will not work. It just will not work.

Many people don't believe that the main problem is the home. That's where it all begins, at home. From home is where everything comes. From home comes community. From home comes churches. Home becomes schools. From home comes government. Everything comes from the home. The school is the next step.

As I told you earlier, the school has a handicap. The school is caught up between the two, and the school has been cut short in opportunity. They prepared themselves, and they are still preparing themselves to do the job. But they are handicapped by other sources of power that have come in. The school board is trying to operate the classroom; that will not work. The government is trying to operate a portion of it; that will not work. The courts are operating the other portion, and we see that will not work. Nobody is in charge. When everybody is trying to be in charge of one thing, it ends up that no one is in charge. It's running loose. It's unstable, and it's nonproductive, because it's in too many hands. Only the teacher can control the classrooms and give the classrooms that for which they were designed, only the teachers. Only the teachers can improve the knowledge of those who are sent there, if they have the opportunity to do so. Only the schools can fill that second portion of life of mankind. Only the schools can do that. Let the schools do so. If this happens with the schools, then the church will be able to play its role more freely.

The failure of the man of God is to warn the home, to place the warning at the doors of the homes. None of these things can be changed. Those who are guilty have to be told about it. Those who are headed in the wrong direction have to be changed. The dangerous situation is out of hand, which has caused the homes to be devoured within themselves and because we have babies having babies. We need these three institutions to come together, the home, the school, and the Church.

SERMON OUTLINES ON THE CHURCH

The Church and the Kingdom

"And I say also unto thee, That thou art Peter, and upon this rock I will build my church; and the gates of hell shall not prevail against it." (St. Matthew 16:18)

This is Jesus talking to His disciples and revealing the mysteries of the Church, and this is the New Testament Church that we preach today. As Jesus was in the midst of his teaching, and touring the land of Palestine, He came to the Sea of Caesarea Philippi, and He questioned His disciples concerning Him. Now Jesus knew what they knew, and He knew what they knew about him and what they thought about Him. But He didn't question them because He didn't know. He questioned them because they didn't know, and because of what they had heard or what the people said was not the true identity of what He was going to reveal unto them.

He asked them the question, "Whom do men say that I the son of man am?" And they said, "Some say thou art John the Baptist: some say Elijah, and others, Jeremiah, or one of the prophets." (Matthew 16:13-14) So that was the summary of what some said, and he brought the question up to them by saying, "But whom say ye that I am?" or who do you say that I am? And Simon Peter answered and said, "Thou art the Christ, the Son of the living God." That's in the sixteenth verse of Matthew's Gospel. And Jesus answered and let him know this insight didn't come from flesh and blood, but it was "revealed unto thee by my Father which is in heaven." That's in the seventeenth verse of Matthew. Jesus had to remind Peter, and Peter was not ready to receive such information from Him. He was not prepared. Peter was unsaved. Peter's life had not been changed. Peter couldn't see such information being placed in his future. So, Jesus had to let him know that he didn't speak that "out of the depths of your heart, but it came by revelation by God".

This reminds us of when the people are sitting out in the audience where we are preaching to them. They hear it, but they don't understand it, because they are not prepared to understand such a message from God. They will have to be people of repentance and people who have been filled with the Holy Spirit and their lives changed before they can understand what the preacher is preaching. They sit there, not because they are benefiting, but because it's Sunday morning. Their intelligence told them to be present. I think that we should understand that to receive the word, your vessel must be in receiving order, and that means in God, and having a new mind and a right spirit. Notice the attitude of Peter. Notice how casual he was in dealing with this situation. You don't find him excited. You don't find him enthusiastic, not even dismayed. (But normally, someone would have said something that someone had told him what and how to say it.) If someone told you that God was speaking to you, or through you, that should have brought some enthusiasm or some reaction just to know that God had spoken through you. But Peter showed no sign, no interest, in what Jesus had said. Peter's mind was focused on what he had imagined was going to take place in the future. He saw Jesus as the king, who was coming to set up His earthly kingdom. Peter was not too concerned about what the kingdom would be like or of what the kingdom consisted. He was more interested in Jesus being king on the throne. So, until some signs would move His imagination, He had nothing to bring excitement unto Him. He was not moved, or lifted, because he was told that this truth had been revealed unto him. He just listened to it without giving an amen, or praise God. He just heard it and kept his position as he was.

This moved the evidence from the people's thought of him as not being the prophet that they were anticipating him being. He was the Christ, the Son of the living God. His disciples were not too well rehearsed in their low key of understanding. They considered that He was the Messiah, the one whom they understood from prophecy would come and save the people. They were not understanding that He would save them by dying for them instead and rising for their justification. All of this would take place by Him presiding on an earthly throne.

The answer to what some say, I know what others say, is that it established what Peter said because it was revealed to him by God.

That thou art the Christ, the Son of the living God. As He continued on, he told them that he would follow this truth. He said in the eighteenth verse: "Thou art Peter, and upon this rock I will build my church." Please underline this. He said, "I will build my church, and the gates of hell shall not prevail against it." Now, he said "I will build," not now but I will; not here, but I will. This has been a conjunction in our lives, and has brought about a blockade to our preaching concerning salvation, and that is the Church. With that saying, "I will build my church," we fail to understand that the word build makes us feel like the Church is built instead of being born.

Now the Church is built. There is a difference in the Lord building and man building. When man speaks of building, he's thinking of modern bricks and a hammer and nails, but the Lord builds with spirit and power. The building of the Church brings too many forces of God together to understand a human being born. It brings life together, and all the major participants of life are brought in to one in God's way of building. He builds his Church through the birth of the Church.

Anything that has life is born. Things that are not born do not have life. There, to have life it has to be born. The Church is a living being; it has life because it was born. We will be dealing with this in the next outline.

Let us understand. Let's look at Peter, one of the disciples who proved to be the spokesman of the group, and one who was called upon and who preached most of the day. He could be misleading, because to know of Peter's conversion and the Peter of the call of Christ, you must understand the difference between these two Peters. This Peter to whom Jesus was speaking in this situation was the Peter who was called and commissioned to follow Him so that He would make him a fisher of men. He did not promise him at the time that He would be an evangelist. He didn't promise him at the time that he would be a writer or a bishop. He promised only, "Follow me, and I will make you fishers of men." (St. Matthew 4:19) Jesus knew that Peter would not remember the things that He was telling him at the present time. He had also told him that He wouldn't remember it and that these things would be brought to his memory when the time was right. At this time, he could not. He could not remember, and he didn't have the spiritual life or the interest in being lifted up and having an enthusiastic attitude. The good news that was given to him was not so good because it did not measure up to the theory and imagination that he had about the future.

He had his mind set on modernizing the kingdom of Israel, and the difference would be that it would be run differently because the king would be different. The king would be Jesus. He could not highly appreciate that Jesus would build this Church on what He said. How could it be such a joyful occasion to be there when he really didn't know what it was? He heard him say Church, but he didn't know what it was. How do you expect Peter to know what the Church was when two thousand years later, you have people who don't know what the Church is? They don't know the difference between the Church and the house of God where the Church worships. Peter had a true reason to be in his condition, but we should know better. We should know the difference between the Church and the house of God. So what did Peter know about building the Church on this sand or building it anywhere? He didn't know anything about any Church. At this time he couldn't hold this truth sacred because he was filled with fear before God. He didn't even say it, and we have no way of knowing if he believed it or not, because he didn't say anything or show anything, and it was just in the making.

What we have in the word tells us how Jesus announced how the Church would be built. His speech concerning the Church meant that the Church would be conceived. And if you know the Scripture, from this time the Church begins to grow in the ministry of Christ. That was the only place it could grow, because Jesus was the only one who knew about the Church. Jesus said very little in his earthly ministry concerning the Church, but he talked a lot about the Church as a kingdom.

That's our problem today. We have totally dismissed the idea or understanding of the Kingdom and set up the Church on our own theory and understanding. That's why it's ineffective. It's unspiritual, and it has become a social gathering, producing nothing. We must take the lesson from the life of Peter. If Peter were blessed with salvation, with the Holy Spirit, with the leadership of God through his Holy Spirit that we experience, I'm sure Peter would have had a better attitude, a better spiritual attitude, than what he had then. He became that different Peter after the Church was born. Peter acted and lived as the Church when it was born in him. We are living like Peter when he received this message, cold and without understanding, without any enthusiasm. As Peter was then, that's the way we are now. We have no excuse for that. So then, Jesus said, "I will build my church and the gates of hell shall not prevail against it." How much did Peter know about Hell, what Hell would do and the kind of opposition that Hell would have against the Church when he didn't know what it was? We're suppose to know. We're suppose to deal with situations, because we have the Lord's promises that Hell will not destroy the Church. Hell would not prevail. It can't stay there, it has to move. There are too many problems in the Church that move in and stay through generations simply because we don't practice that church force, that togetherness, and that praising attitude, that separates us from the world.

Jesus explained to Peter that He was going to build it, and He would always remember because the truth had been told about who He was His and what His presence was all about. He went on, telling him in the nineteenth verse, "And I will give unto thee the keys of the kingdom." He didn't say Church; He said, "Kingdom of Heaven: and whatsoever thou shalt bind on Earth shall be bound in Heaven: and whatsoever thou shalt loose on Earth shall be loosed in Heaven." Even speaking of the authority, and the power, that's what the "key" means. That didn't lift Peter. That didn't change Peter's attitude; it didn't cause him to think of leaping for joy because he was given these things.

What you don't understand can't mean too much to you. What you don't understand, you can't use. Peter couldn't see himself in the position of exercising anything to do with "keys" and "binding in the Earth as it is in Heaven." All this information goes in this work of this authority. He couldn't understand that. He wasn't ready for the understanding. He didn't need to understand, because the Church was not going to be built there in Caesarea Philippi. It was not going to be built with the sensibility of mankind, the materialistic world. It could not be built according to God's plan while Jesus was in the midst of His earthly ministry as the Son of God. The Church could not function at the same time that Jesus was here as the Son of God. The Church couldn't function because it didn't have anything with which to function. As long as Jesus was in his earthly ministry as the Son of God, the Church didn't have room because the Church was not born. The church hadn't been brought into existence.

Peter was a follower. Peter was a chosen one; he answered the call. Now, mind you, when Jesus called these brethren, He promised to make them better at what they were doing. That's what they knew about. Their trade was fishing. Their living was fishing. They knew fishing. Jesus didn't oppose what they were doing, but He said, "I'll make you catch more than what you are catching." He didn't tell them they wouldn't fish anymore. He just said, "Not only will you catch fish, but you will also catch men. Men will be your occupation, and when you learn how to catch them, then it will determine when you want to fish for fish or when you want to fish for men. He was giving them the information about where men might be caught. They knew the places to catch the fish, but to Catch men, the Church would have to be involved in the world.

The world doesn't come into the Church; the Church goes out into the world. When a man goes fishing, the water does not come to him, he goes to the water. He doesn't go there and jump into the water to catch the fish. He goes there with the techniques to catch the fish. So it is with the men of the Church. You don't go out there and get in the world to catch a man, but you have the techniques to go to the world. You go to the world to catch the man and bring him from the world to the Church.

When you look at the situation at the time Jesus was teaching and look at whom He was teaching and what He was teaching about, then we get the full understanding; then we will be able to keep everything in proper perspective.

Now, sadly to say, many of our pastors hardly ever go out into the world to catch men; they wait in the house of God until men take a notion to come to them. Well, if you can do that, then you should just sit at home and wait for the fish to leave the water to come to you. If you have to go to the sea or the lake to catch the fish, don't you think you will have to go to the world to catch men? Or do you think they should come out of the world and come to you because you see it that way? That's a poor result, and what have we experienced? We experience that time is wasted, because the only new people that most congregations receive are from other congregations. When men are troubled and run out of opportunities and turn and come seeking the Church, it's like a person on fire who is seeking to be put out. He wouldn't have come if trouble, or sickness, or something unfortunate hadn't happened. Then, he is comes to the Church because someone told him things can be changed with the Church.

Let us remember that Peter didn't understand the message. He didn't understand what Jesus was telling him, but it registered in his mind so that when the time came it would be brought forth and given to him. He couldn't understand all that was given to him. He couldn't understand, and Peter didn't say a word. Don't you think he should have been able to say amen, praise the Lord, or thank you for giving me these positions? But he didn't say a word. As we note (the continuation was before they got any distance) from all this excitement, Jesus began to tell them. He told them, and the Scripture says in St. Matthew 16:20: "Then charged he his disciples that they should tell no man that He was Jesus the Christ." Now Jesus said don't tell anyone that I'm the Christ for many reasons. They won't believe you. You didn't believe it, and you still don't believe it. You say it because it was revealed to you. And the rest of you heard when I made it known and revealed to Peter. So there is no way you can explain to them your evidence for knowing that I'm the Christ, so just tell no man. Don't cause them to interrupt my ministry and plans. So just tell no man that I am the Christ, because they will not seek me as Christ. They will seek me as an enemy.

The people were not seeking Christ to be saved or to be spiritually strengthened, but they were only concerned about what He could do for them. He could feed them, or He could heal them, or, maybe, He could protect them. Those who didn't believe were in opposition. They were jealous. They wanted to do away with Him. They felt their kingdom was threatened, their kingdom was coming to an end, so they strictly opposed Him. He charged them saying, "Don't tell anyone that I'm the Christ." Amen. Don't tell anyone, no man, that Jesus is the Christ. And they began to notice, and Peter quietly went along with the rest. In that twenty-first verse of St. Matthew it says "From that time forth began Jesus to shew unto his disciples, how that He must go unto Jerusalem, and suffer many things of the elders and chief priests and scribes, and be killed, and be raised again the third day."

Jesus begin to show them what would take place. Now this was not the first time that Jesus had told them that. He would tell them that His departure was near. This was in a crucial time, because it had renewed the earthly idea of His disciples that things were looking better on Earth and their wishes were beginning to turn in their favor—that He was coming closer to setting up the Kingdom, that this kingdom would represent Heaven instead of some other ruler or some other harem of Caesar, that the kingdom where Jesus would preside would represent Heaven. This was a time when they were focusing on what they thought.

It's very difficult to get the word over to people or to get anything over to people when they have already made up their minds, set their standard, and come to a conclusion in their minds about a situation. It is hard to get the truth to them. It is hard to get them to think any other way except what they have in their minds. It's a true saying that it's one thing when we learn the condition of not knowing, then we begin to improve ourselves in our condition, because when we realize we don't know, that's not enough. We must realize that we need to know. That's not enough. We need to realize to know. We must learn better, and that's not enough. We must realize we cannot learn and know at the same time. Amen. Amen.

Something to Remember

"And the Lord turned, and looked upon Peter. And Peter remembered the word of the Lord, how he had said unto him, Before the cock crow, thou shalt deny me thrice." (St. Luke 22:61) Now this is the coming to conclusion of the earthly ministry of the Son of God, as Jesus began to be transformed into the works of redemption, and His Kingdom He came to begin. He had finished His ministry of preaching and teaching throughout the territory where He preached, taught, worked, and performed miracles of all kinds.

He had led His disciples through a long night of watching while He prayed. As the life became dreadful, and the cup was bitter to drink, Jesus showed the impact of the suffering for our sins that He took upon Himself. He lead His disciples through these periods that they might understand and be able to preach it after He was gone. Jesus preached the Kingdom while He was on Earth. He preached what the Kingdom would be. He preached that He would build it and of what it would consist. The Church would be inserted into Israel instead of the Kingdom. The Kingdom would become the Church, and the Church would become the Kingdom.

He began the darkest period of His ministry, and all the work was His. He did the work Himself. He called His disciples to follow Him, not to work but to see Him, to hear Him, and to witness Him while He worked. So the time was coming, and He began to certify His own work. He was certified through His suffering and His suffering began. It began with the night of prayer, of seeking to have the cup changed. The human side of Christ began to rise to the occasion. This torch, the unbearable pain and suffering, and the cry was made in the garden, "If there was any other way for this cup to pass, and thy will be done."

We notice that the first and second time He made this prayer He received no answer. The third time that He went, He prayed the prayer and gave His own answer: "Thy will be done. Thy will; it's not my will." And He finally decided to awake them for the final time, and it was time for suffering to begin.

The crowd of his enemies was waiting at the entrance of the garden so that He might be betrayed by one of His own brethren.

This kind of situation should not be demonstrated in our lifetime, because our brethren are supposed to be as one. There should not be any betrayal among us. There should not be any broken links. There should be true and strong fellowship with one another.

The time had come for Peter not to speak this time, but to demonstrate the things he had spoken concerning Christ and to stand for them. Peter was in the same condition he was before, weak and unaware of what was happening. And his idea of protecting the Kingdom of Christ was not his way. As He came in, Jesus was identified by Judas, one of the brethren to whom he gave a life position among others. Judas chose to use it for his own well-being, and he betrayed his love with a kiss.

Then it began. Jesus allowed Himself to present himself. He presented himself in an intelligent and a divine attitude. He gave them enough of His power to let them know that He understood His own power of humbleness, because He first performed a miracle by Peter, who was beginning to be moved. Peter's understanding was to protect Jesus, whatever the cost might be, but he relied on protection by his sword not by his faith. When Jesus began to speak to the crowd about how they came out to Him, as if He were some kind of dangerous outlaw, Peter became so uptight and steamed up in a warfare attitude, He began to swing his sword, and he took off the ear of one of the priests. Jesus healed the ear wound and ordered Peter to put the sword away. So, Peter had to realize his fight was not with a sword, but the victory comes by being humble with the things pertaining to life—something he didn't understand.

Peter had enough courage to follow the mob with Jesus. Who knows what he hoped would come to pass, but he followed them.

That was a frightening time for the disciples, because they were fearful. But Peter—in his physical temper, his madness steadfast in his own strength—followed Jesus as they went to the quarters of the priest for His trial to determine what would be the next step for Jesus to take. Peter came, and since it was cold, Peter made a fire and sat among them. Who can imagine what was in his mind, as he hoped that somehow the situation would change.

It is always something that causes you to take a stand in life. Peter could not go through this period of life untouched, because he was with Jesus.

We who are with Jesus must suffer and bear the same pains. We must suffer for the same cause. Our way of conducting ourselves must be in the same way. The price we have to pay, we must pay it in the same way.

Peter had to experience the charge that he might be able to carry this information, this truth, for a later day. He remained, and as one came in and said, "He's one of them. We know that he's one of them," Peter said, "I know not the man. I know nothing about what you are talking." Peter denied Jesus.

Many of us take it as Peter denied, or Peter didn't tell the truth, but you have a mystery there, because Peter didn't know Jesus. Peter knew of Jesus. Peter knew him on the level of other men. Who knows, he could have known Him on the level of himself. Peter's expectation, because of the power that Christ had demonstrated in His ministry, was that everything would respond to Christ's demand. All He would have to do is say the word, and they would knock all men out.

Peter should not be criticized for thinking that way, because he was thinking as a human being, and that's what he was. What we should understand is why, and why not, he was unable to think like we think today. Peter knew of Christ. He didn't know Jesus. Just like most of us, we congregate and go to our many church houses, but we do not know the Lord. We know of Him. The only way we can know the Lord is by His Spirit. If we are not filled with and familiar with the Holy Spirit, we know nothing of God.

You don't know God through some spooky idea or something that happened. You know Him by His Spirit. The more you know Him by His Spirit, the broader your knowledge in Him becomes. I don't understand how people confess to have the knowledge of God and have not the Spirit of God. There is no other way you can know God except through His Spirit.

If you are not familiar with the Spirit of God, then you are not worthy to know who God is. We know Him by His Spirit. One thing we have to understand. Some people feel as if the Spirit is designed only to make you happy, but the Spirit of God is designed to give you the knowledge to know God. Happiness comes with it. When you know God, then you exist. You live in Him, and you follow His instructions. This is what makes a world better, when people become a part of His great Kingdom, which is the Church. Therefore, Peter didn't have the Spirit. He knew that Jesus was the one who called him. He knew that he had been following Jesus. He knew he saw the works of Jesus. He saw the miracles. He heard Him preach. He heard Him teach, but He was always teaching something that Peter couldn't comprehend. He didn't know what it was; he couldn't remember it. Anything that you can't remember, you can't worry about. You can't use what you can't remember. You can't call a name unless you remember the name. You can't go to a place unless you remember the place, and remember how to get there. You must remember. So, Peter couldn't remember, because he was not seeking for remembrance. He wasn't seeking to understand. What Jesus was teaching had no reference to anything that Peter was seeking.

Peter wasn't seeking the Church. He wasn't seeking the Kingdom. He was being obedient in following Jesus and obeying Jesus for the things that Jesus had told him to do. Peter didn't know Jesus, he knew of Him. He knew Him as the man. He knew Him as believing He was the Messiah, and he could only understand the Messiah as the words of a prophet. Peter didn't know Jesus was God. He didn't know that Jesus was salvation. He didn't know these things. When he was pressed by the enemy that he was one of them, he told what was better for him in a human sense. He feared the harm that would have come upon him. In the human sense, he did deny Him. He said he didn't know Him; he didn't know anything about Him. But he knew the maid said that he was with Him. He denied being with Him. But it didn't matter if he denied that he was with Him. That didn't make him any better or any worse, because he didn't know Him. It didn't make him a worse sinner or a worse unsaved person, because there is nothing worse than being unsaved. You are either saved or unsaved. You are in Christ or you are not. He knew Jesus as following Jesus, by being with Him. But to know Him as life, and that if they took his life that Jesus could restore His life, or preserve His life, he had no way of knowing that. In his physical sense he said, "I don't know Him." I don't even know what you are talking about." Truthfully speaking, he didn't know Him. He didn't know Jesus. He didn't know the plans for the building of the Church. He didn't know that this was in a physical world. This was a sad situation; this was dreadful. And to turn around to life...it was great. It was paying the price that we might be set free. Thank God.

Thank God, because this same Peter had a chance on the other side of life to stand up for what he denied, to live for what he denied, and to die for what he denied. He denied it in the best time. He confessed it in the right time and in the most safe time.

We become confused in our theological preaching to people. We give them the weakness of preaching, and we refrain from preaching the truth, preaching the sound doctrine of Christ and the teaching of Christ. You have the doctrine of Christ, which is the teaching of Christ, and the suffering, death, and resurrection of Christ, which is

His doctrine. We need to know the difference between the history and entertaining people.

We need to seek their lives and help them to discover salvation and to strive for eternity with Christ. This is not being done. We have become so delicate in our preaching and our teaching. We have become so self-controlled and self centered in our intelligence, we have lost sight of the Gospel. Every preacher that is preaching today is not preaching the Gospel. Many times we're rehearsing history; we're telling stories. We have told stories for so long that we call the Gospel a story. The Gospel is not a story. A story is a complete situation, and you can read it over and over and it doesn't increase; it remains the same. The Gospel is a living message, the living Word of God, and every time you speak of it or seek after it, you will find more. It's a living Word, a living message. It's the life.

Peter was caught up in his situation. His survival was to deny, to deny all that the people saw. Peter was denying the man they had bound and who was sitting in the counsel. He was denying the man's appearance. None of the disciples knew that it was God sitting in the midst of them. Instead of them counseling Him (Jesus), they would have been better off if He had counseled them. Peter denied that he knew about Christ and what Christ was saying. It was not salvation; he didn't know enough about Him. That he knew about Him is what he defended. He denied he knew the man in order to escape what was before him. Yes, he denied that he knew Him. Yes, he denied that he knew what they were talking about, but Jesus had already told Peter. When Peter began to express to Jesus how dedicated he was in following Him, He said, "I will go all the way with you, even unto death," Jesus knew at that time man couldn't stand.

Can't you see men today who go on a rampage and kill people, and afterwards they will do anything and everything to try to escape or to try to save their own lives. Man's sense of thinking is so shallow. It's unstable until it's foolish. When a person goes out to destroy life, that means he has a low evaluation of life, and he has a blind view of living. Instead of living one day at a time, he has to live one minute at a time, because he can do more in that minute to destroy life then anyone else can.

Peter, yes he denied Him, but not only was he unable to understand what the words of Christ were leading to, He couldn't even remember the things Christ told him. He knew that everything obeyed the words of Jesus when Jesus spoke. It didn't matter what

He spoke to, water, trees, diseases, death, or whatever. When Jesus spoke, they all obeyed. They did what He said. In the midst of all this, Peter could not remember Christ saying. "Before the cock crows, you will deny me." Peter could not remember that, because he had no thoughts. He had no reason to seek these kinds of things for memories. He didn't see anywhere for them to be used in his life.

When people have to stand off and imagine what the Church is like, and use their imagination, they don't see room in their life for any kind of Church or plans for salvation. When they look at their life it's already filled. They have already filled it with something. Some have filled it with money, some have filled it on credit, and some have just filled it up with nothing. They just want to stand by the wayside and whatever comes my way.

You have to seek to find something worthwhile, something to complete your life You have to believe and have a Lord to look to and have direction by the Holy Spirit in order to fill up the emptiness in life.

So Peter didn't have this. Peter used only what he had. He had been told that whenever he had spoken, denying the truth, it was not him speaking, but it was Him that was speaking in him. As he sat by the fire, and others looked upon him, and said, "This man was also with Him,"(St. Luke 22:56 and 57) Peter denied Jesus by saying, "Woman I knew him not." True. He of him.

How many people in your congregation know of Christ? How many in the pulpit know of Him? How many people from anywhere know of Christ and really don't know Him? If you don't know Him in your life, then you don't know Him. It's leading you to His ministry, or through His time, and through His plans. If you don't know Him through His Spirit, you don't know Him. Anyone who can confess Christ should be able to tell the works of the Holy Spirit within him. In verse fifty-nine. there is another who came, affirmed, saying, "Of a truth this fellow was also with him, for he is a Galilaean." Peter said, "I know not what thou sayest. And immediately, while he yet spake, the cock crew." As he denied him, the Lord turned and looked upon Peter.

The Lord knew how to get Peter's attention, and when he turned, that struck Peter's memories of what Jesus had said. That caused Peter to remember what Jesus had told him. In that text it says, "The Lord turned and looked upon Peter, and Peter remembered the word of the Lord, how he had said unto him, 'Before the cock crow, thou shall deny me thrice.'" (Luke 22:60 and 61) That was something Peter remembered. That was something that was placed at the order of him. Peter forgot what Jesus had said, but he never forgot the crowing of the rooster. The crowing of the rooster was on the same terms as the language of Peter; he could remember that. He couldn't remember what Jesus had said. When the rooster crowed, it struck him; it moved him. You'll see understanding, and when you understand what He said, when you understand what it's about, it has a physical and human reaction, as well as a spiritual action.

When Peter was in the midst of those questioning him, why couldn't he remember what Jesus had told him? What Jesus had told him was not on the level of the rooster crowing. The rooster crowing was on a visible level, where Peter could understand. But when Jesus told him about what would happen between now and midnight, he could not remember that. When Jesus called him to remember by turning and looking upon him, that had a great impact upon Peter. According to the text, when the Lord turned and looked upon him, Peter remembered the words, "Before the cock crows, thou shall deny me thrice." And Peter went out and wept bitterly because he remembered.

The men held Jesus, mocking him. Jesus was inside receiving punishment and abuse from His enemy, and Peter was outside wrestling with the memories that were brought to him by the rooster.

I think we should be careful how we keep these, or scramble this information and lay it out so we can understand. You will have to serve the Lord on your level. You'll have to serve Him with your language and serve Him with your understanding. You have to serve Him with what you have. You cannot serve Him with what you don't have. That means we have to be born of the Church. We have to have the Church working in us in order for us to be the people of that Church. That Church must be in us, and it is in us. Only those born of the Spirit of God have received the presence of that Kingdom built in us. The ministry of the Church is our lives. It's what is keeping us in the building of the Kingdom of our Lord.

So, Peter's demonstration let us know that without Christ, we can do nothing. Without Him, we can learn nothing, because if you don't learn about Him through His Spirit, life has an emptiness and there's no hope for it.

But seek, study to show yourself approved, listen to the preacher, and listen to the minister as he preaches the Gospel. Let it apply in your life. Your life will be transformed by the newness of your mind. Don't try to pattern your life by the Peter who denied Christ but as the Peter who died for Christ's word. If this happens, we will have eternal life through Jesus Christ. We'll be able to live for Him and worship Him. But first we must be born of the Holy Spirit and filled with the Holy Spirit. At this time, the Lord will establish the Kingdom, which is the Church in your heart. You will make life meaningful by having Christ in your life, by being kind and fruitful to each other, and by being part of a great fellowship in the Lord. Amen. Amen.

Wait on the Promises

"And being assembled together with them, commanded them that they should not depart from Jerusalem, but wait for the promise of the Father which saith he, Ye have heard of me. For John truly baptized with water; but ye shall be baptized with the Holy Ghost not many days hence." (Acts 1:4-5)

Jesus appeared unto the disciples after his resurrection, probably to bring their attention to some of the events that they had seen and heard concerning Him. This is the ingredient of the Church that is brought together to generate the power of the almighty God, to establish the Church in the hearts of men and women. The Lord God had promised this power would come to pass and be experienced by those who were chosen by Jesus Himself. The disciples had become closer to becoming the disciples that were in the making from the providence of God. Jesus and only Jesus was their teacher; no one else had the ability or the privilege to even attempt to teach them anything. He began to let them know, "What I have taught you concerning the promises of my father will soon be at hand," and you will be the ones to be involved. You are the ones to receive the results and to explain the necessity of them having it. By telling them not to depart from Jerusalem. (Jerusalem is the capital of the land of Caanan, and the plan and purpose for the church to be born). Bring the attention and emerge in the minds of His followers that John truly baptized with water, but ye shall be baptized with the Holy Ghost, not many days hence. It was very important for them to receive and to identify in faith what Jesus was teaching them. But when they experience these powers, the mighty change will take place in their lives as they develop in divine beliefs of Christ. They had to be reminded and instructed that they could not receive this gift, this power no where else, except Jerusalem. In this text, God didn't reveal many details concerning the events as they unfold, but His plans were for them to be present and understand, so when it unfolds in their minds and in their lives. So to receive this, they must be at the proper place, at the appointed time.

This is why it is so important for men and women to listen to the Word of God and listen to the Gospel of Jesus Christ so that they may be able to be prepared when the Lord brings about changes in their lives and be able to recognize that the Lord is dealing with them.

It had to be this way, since the Church is not built with mortar bricks or with things for the kind of kingdom which with the people were familiar. This was new; this was going to be not only a new kingdom, but a new life that would completely change their lives from old things to new. This would commission them to become partakers of the alter of this divine purpose.

That is why the Lord keeps His own providence in the power to call, to ordain, and to send His ministers, not leave it in the hands of anyone else. But, on the other hand, the disciples were confused and were unable to understand what Jesus was telling them, because their minds were fixed on the idea that Jesus was going to set up an earthly kingdom. In verse six, they asked Him a question: "When they therefore were come together, they asked of Him saying, 'Lord, wilt thou at this time restore again the kingdom to Israel?'" Verse seven: "And He said unto them, 'It is not for you to know the times or the seasons, which the Father hath put in His own power.'" Verse eight: "But ye shall receive power after that the Holy Ghost is come upon you: and ye shall be witnesses unto me both in Jerusalem and in all Judaea, and in Samaria, and unto the uttermost part of the earth." Their assumption was that Jesus was going to set up or restore this kingdom back to Israel, but He, Jesus, would be on the throne. They considered in their minds if Jesus would be king, they would remain His disciples. Not only were His disciples under that impression, but many others. Occasionally, there were some who tried to force Him to be their king.

We must understand that the kingdom of Israel was replaced by the Church. Jesus's Kingdom was never to be built as other Kingdoms. There's a difference in what the Lord builds and what carpenters build. When carpenters build, they build with a hammer, nails, mortar, and bricks. When the Lord builds, it's life. It's a living building, a living kingdom. Whatever He builds is living.

It has come to pass as He promised, "That I will build my church and the gates of hell shall not prevail against it." He continued saying to them, that the answer to your question about what I will do with the kingdom is in the power of my father. You will receive that after the Holy Ghost has come upon you. When you receive it, you will understand. You will have the power to realize where the Kingdom will be built, because it will be built in you and others.

As you know, Jesus said very little concerning the Church in the Church's name. He called the name Church a very few times, but He spoke of the Kingdom many many times. He taught concerning the

Kingdom and why you can't understand. He was talking about the function, how the Church would function when it came to pass. That means after it was born. He built the Church in the hearts of men and women, to everyone who believes. Everyone who repents and accepts Christ receives the power of the Holy Spirit. The Holy Spirit and the power of the Church come in the same package. When you received the Holy Ghost, you have received the Church because the Church is established in your hearts. You can only be the Church because the Holy Spirit is the life of the Church. Many times we recognize a strange feeling, and we call it, "happy" or "the spirit." But we are blind with the idea that that is the Church, and the life of the Church is the Holy Spirit. Thank God that later the disciples experienced what the Lord had told them. This was experienced in their lives and opened their understanding. That's why when they were filled with the Holy Spirit, He brought all things to their memories. They didn't just talk or shout about it; they acted accordingly.

In this question and answering period between Jesus and His disciples, he established the fact that the church was in the making, and Jesus was about ready to return to His throne, and the disciples were on their way to their waiting place for the arrival of the church. We talk about it, in parts, we talk about the waiting for the Holy Spirit, the ten days waiting for the Holy Spirit. We failed to included that the church was in the same package. Those who waited, the apostles along with the one hundred and twenty members. They were waiting and witnessing to become the instrument to receive the experience, the birth of the church. It is clear to us today, that we have overlooked, by rushing through the scriptures, and coming to the conclusion of our own ideas concerning the scriptures. We fail to recognize and the church is missing in our understanding, and it is lost to most people between the house of God and themselves. Many people have lived and died, not knowing the difference between the New Testament Church, and the house of God. The church has dwelled in many people and they have done the best they could which was limited because they failed to recognize the church working in them, or the church function was in them. They believe that the evidence of the church is the material activities that we carry on in the house of God which is made of our own. That's why we have so many different activities going on in the house of God. Ml kinds of program, and all kinds of rallies and all kinds of banquets, all kinds of carrying on as the world is carrying on in order to entertain, to keep the mind focused on returning back. People live and die believing that you have to always return back to the house of God to feel or to act according to results of the church. It plainly tells us that the kingdom of our Lord is established in our hearts. Until we recognize and understand what it is, we fail to follow the leadership in our lives and in our homes, and the world suffers because of that great failure.

If the building of the kingdom, which is built by us because it is in us, could have it's proper time and opportunity in our lives, the world wouldn't be overshadowed by the corruption of the minds of men and women, and especially young people. It has come to pass that young people minds are so corrupted. Many of them are not living to see the age of thirty because they have nothing to live for. It is certain that if you have nothing to live by, you can't have something to live for. When we try to make it without the leadership and the guidance of our Creator that means we will soon run out. We grow faster than the world can manufacture new titles and new ways for destruction. We see this evidence when we congregate in the house of God, that we have to use formalities or ways to entertain. The choirs have to keep us from going to sleep. After they finish singing and trying to keep us from going to sleep, they sit down and the minister gets up, then they go to sleep. Simply because it's an entertainment situation. When you are entertained, it lasts as long as the music lasts, when the music stop, our entertainment stops and we soon become bored in whatever is going on. The church is not the house, the church is not designed for entertainment. He said when you receive this power ye shall be witnesses unto me. That means we are witnesses to each other and witnesses to those that know not Him. Even witnessing for Jesus is life itself It's a joy to realize the privileges, and to be the instrument of God, and controlled by His presence and by His Holy Spirit. All the promises of life and all the ingredients that He has compiled in His kingdom and in our lives will never allow us to have a boring moment especially in the house of God.

Jesus had given them the plans and outlines, and, at the same time, the disciples were in a little better condition to listen to what He was saying, because this was taking place after the resurrection of Christ. He had visited these brethren before. He had breathed on them, and they were filled with the Holy Ghost. But they were still on the long list of waiting. They didn't have the enthusiasm, because they had not yet received the power. The Holy Ghost was the gift and is the gift that is given to every believer. And the Church came through power. The disciples, the twelve, had the Holy Ghost even when they were waiting. They were waiting for the power of the promises, which was the Church to come. This time, that's why they received the charge from the Lord not to leave Jerusalem. This was the plan and the purpose of God. There is something about Jerusalem. God has always visited His people, whatever way He visited them, at or around Jerusalem. In spite of the danger and the fear that they had for their lives, Jesus said wait. He knew of the danger under which they were living. He knew how dangerous it was for them to even speak in His name, but He said, "Wait." He didn't give them the time or the hour of how long it would take, but He said don't leave Jerusalem until you endure with power. If you understand, He said, don't witness. Don't begin to witness until you receive the power, because if you start to witness, you don't know anything about which to witness. You don't have the full truth or understanding, or the message of the promises to know what to witness about until you wait and receive power so that you'll be able to tell what has arrived and how to explore every soul that will trust and believe on the Lord.

This was something new. You cannot witness and explain something you don't know yourself. It would have been impossible for them to witness this building of the Kingdom without knowing what the Kingdom was. The disciples focused upon the earthly kingdom. They had not yet understood, in spite of Jesus telling them over and over, that He would be taken and He would leave them and return back to His Father. They couldn't understand that; they couldn't receive that, because they had already made up their minds and were holding to their understanding of the type of kingdom they knew about.

We can be caught up in the same thing, and we are caught up in the same thing when we get the answer fixed in our minds our ways. Most times, listening to the truth never reaches us or never changes us. We are our own witnesses, sometimes even in wrong. And it is very dangerous to become the witness of you, within yourself, on something about which you are wrong. That is very dangerous and very hopeless in life. This was the situation that was among the brethren who were following Jesus. They understood so little as He taught them to be the men who would reach out and fish for men.

He instructed them to wait in Jerusalem, to stay there. They would get all the answers to every question. They would get a clear picture of His Kingdom. His Kingdom would possess them. They would become the temple of the Kingdom that they would preach, and they would declare the message of that Kingdom.

Isn't it strange today that we have so many, so many churches, as we say. We call every building the Church in the time now when church buildings are being burned down and destroyed. Our hearts go out to the people in those communities. It's a sad day when someone tries to burn down the house of God. But no one can burn the Church. Fire cannot burn the Church. No one can start a fire in the Church. The Church has its own fire, and the fire that burns within the Church is not the type of fire that burns down buildings. It has it source of burning within. The cleansing, the desires, and the things that consist in life shouldn't be there. The fire that burns the church house destroys it. When you burn something, you burn all the substance out of it. This fire in the church, it purifies when it burns. Fire destroys what should be burned and should be removed—the stains, the softness, the disappointment that we lag within. The fire that is in the Church burns away whatever it burns. It purifies and makes it worthy and clean before God. It is not the physical fire that burns down the house of God.

The people who are doing this are very sick. They think they are hurting whoever they are trying to hurt, but they are hurting themselves. The only way they can burn the people is if the people are in the house. But they burn down the empty houses, thinking they are burning the Church. They are fooling themselves. You cannot burn the Church. The Church was demonstrated long ago. Before any buildings were built, God had people walk in the midst of fire that could destroy them. The physical fire couldn't burn them. They represented the presence of God, the God who is unburnable. You can't burn God, and you can't burn the Church; He is the life of the Church. Jesus is the head of the Church; therefore, you cannot burn the Church. Nobody can burn the church.

Maybe this is to get our attention, and maybe there's too much going on in the house of God that's insulting God. Many people spend a lot of time at the house of God and grow so little. When we think about our time and the activities that are going on in God's houses, do we ever think about how much God is accepting? How much is God glorified in our action? How much true praising of God and how much true witnessing is being don? How many times do we speak the truth in the house of God? Do we really truthfully mean what we say? Are we convinced, or are we living by hope on what we are doing? I think we need to question ourselves. If we do that, we will soon understand that something is wrong with the practice of our salvation.

I think we should think about our destiny, and, from our actions how we carry on. We practice anything in the house of God. People can live in the world and be the worst people in the community, but when they die, we will bring a celebration into the house of God. We want the preacher, the whole staff, and all the people of the congregation to be there and render a full service to someone who cared nothing about the house of God. Do you think that that's a pleasure before God? Or is that a shame before God? Because when you take people through the house of God, and they are not part of the activities that go on there in the house, that means you are taking advantage of that person because they are dead and they cannot help themselves. That means you are certifying whatever they are. If they are liars and enemies against God, why do you want to bring God's enemies into His house just because they are dead.

So, think about it. His Church is His Kingdom, and His Kingdom is His Church. If we are not the Church, we do not have a Church, because we are the people who are set apart to be the Church.

Amen. Amen.

Why Look Up? He's Coming Back

And while they looked steadfastly toward heaven as he went up, behold, two men stood by them in white apparel; which also said, Ye men of Galilee, why stand ye gazing up into heaven? This same Jesus which is taken up from you into heaven, shall so come in like manner as ye have seen him go into heaven. (Acts 1:10-11)

As Jesus completed His instruction to His disciples, they saw Him being taken up. As He had spoken and began to be taken up, they saw the clouds receive Him out of their sight.

When you think about this, you think about these brethren experiencing the mighty works of God in their own presence. They were able to see their Lord vanish into the heavens. Certainly that fascinated them as they were looking at the way they saw Him go.

It was another time when the angels were used in the earthly ministry of Christ; these two men stood by and reminded them that they had been well informed many times that He would be taken up and departed out of their sight, and the time had come. They had no way to imagine how this would take place. They had nothing to establish an image in their minds to even try to visualize how this would take place. But in this eleventh verse, He says: "Ye men of Galilee, why stand ye gazing up into heaven? This same Jesus, which is taken up from you into heaven, shall so come in like manner as ye have seen him go into heaven."

So, suppose these messengers had not appeared to remind them what Jesus had told them and reminded them early on to go back to Jerusalem? If this had not taken place, who knows if they would have ever remembered what He had told them. Who knows how deep was their looking up in the last moments of seeing Him vanish before their eyes. They would have settled on some kind of religious tale or testimony that would have been established in their minds and which they would have worshipped the rest of their lives. The Lord would not have allowed that to happen to them. He wouldn't have waited until they settled down, returned to their homes, went fishing, or anything else. But while they were gazing, while they were looking up, He interrupted them through an amazing view that they had looking at their master vanishing through the clouds. He didn't allow this amazing sight to build any testimony or idea for them to leave there. But, the men in white apparel (angels) asked them a question, "Why are you standing looking?" You are not acting according to His instruction. He instructed you to do something else. You will not accomplish the mission that He has given you by looking up—all the works and charges He has given you. There is no place where He instructed you to spend your time looking up.

Many times we are caught up in some kind of magic in our lives. On the thrill of it, we build a testimony and become so enthusiastic in our lives until we place our hope and build our hope in ourselves, and soon we become believers ourselves. That's why it's so important for us to hear the Gospel preached as often as we can and every opportunity that we can. Listen to the Word. Whenever the Word is preached, try and be there. Get your mind off the messenger, and get the message because in the Gospel that is being preached, you'll find instruction for your life. You'll find the answer to the questions that have been placed in your mind, the answers to the problems, the answers to the hardship, the answers and the instruction for your tomorrow through the Gospel that is being preached. That is why it's so important that we who are preaching the Gospel preach the Gospel of Jesus Christ and nothing else. All of these answers and promises come from the Word of God that is preached. If God has sent us, then we are held responsible for the successes or the falls, whichever we are the cause.

Therefore, these brethren were unable to consolidate themselves out there for a period of time, to build monuments or alters, or find something upon which to focus their lives. This is where we saw Him go up. Looking up was serving no purpose. Looking up was not following the instructions that had been given. And the question was, why are you standing here? You have been instructed what to do and how to do it. All what your Lord has told you to do, He didn't say do it here. Why stand there gazing, and looking up. They said that same Jesus, not another, but that same Jesus that they saw going up, is coming again in like manner. He's coming in the same mysterious way.

The disciples had no way of understanding what way He would come, because they had not yet accomplished that which the Holy Ghost would bring to them—the memory of their experiences of Christ's teachings and their following Him. One thing, they were obedient to those two men. The angels of the Lord reminded them that the time they were using was being wasted just looking up.

I keep thinking how long would they have kept looking, and what would the results be? What would they have finalized, and would there have been the danger of them settling with some kind of idle thought? Instead of worshipping their tomorrows, they would have spent their time worshipping yesterday. But He spoke, reminding them of the mission before them, the works before them.

You're going to have to experience your journey without Him walking before you. You will have to experience the transition of Him to you. That can't happen while you're standing there looking up. That was a very important period in their lives—to see what Jesus had promised them the three years that they had been following Him. He would be taken away. He would go back to His Father, back to His throne. They would do greater things, as they had seen Him do. But just think about the things that happen in our lives, especially the handworks of God. It's such a mystery; it does something when we are privileged to witness, to be there.

I would be willing to say that many people today haven't had a chance to witness or testify to this fear of the Lord in their lives—that they stop looking at something spectacular they saw in their minds that was so godly, so great, until they realized it was the works of God beyond man's ability.

They just took it for granted that this was taking me in. I know I've been completely changed, not thinking, you're not converted, you're not changed by what you see. You don't grow in grace by what you see or by what you look at. Your faith does not come by looking, it comes by hearing. Many times we spend our lives reacting and believing only what we can see not realizing many times we see things that are not there. You see many things, you see certain signs or certain images of things from a distance, and as you get closer, they will identity themselves to be two or three different objects. When you really get there to see what it is, it's nothing. So your eyes can play tricks on you. The only way your eyes can give you facts is when truth is involved. Now if you can see the truth of what you are looking at, then your eyes can give you pretty good witnessing evidence. But it has to be the truth. You can see good things happening, but you can't see enough of them to change you one way or the other just by seeing it. You've got to do more than see, even if it is good, something that you are really seeking. It's going to take more than just looking, more than just a look for it to have any affect upon you.

These angels knew that this was a dangerous situation. These brethren were caught up in such attraction, because what they were looking at was worth looking at. But when they could no longer see Him, that's when the false establishment could have taken place. He had gone through the clouds, and their looks could not have dealt with their imaginations. They would have taken it as a gift from Him, as He was going up. So, they said, don't think about it, or don't stand here and gaze at Him going up. Do what He said. Go where He said to go, and do what He has told you to do. They didn't seem to be too alarmed by these two men dressed in white and not accompanying their group. They were busy looking up. They did listen to what He had said.

Isn't it amazing how soon He had told them? He would prepare them and make them become witnesses of Him and to Him so soon after. The Scripture says, when He had finished speaking to them, He was taken up then. That means that the echo should have still been sounding in their ears and in their minds that they would receive power. But what they saw placed these promises. They put these promises on hold. It took the angels of the Lord to interrupt their looking up and their concentration to call an end to what could have caused a failure in their mission that was given to them by the Lord.

Well, that happens in our lives today. You have many good people, brethren in missions and deacons of the church who experience some spiritual impact or some enlightenment to brighten their talents and to make them stronger in their gifts and what they are doing. If they are holy deacons, they can cooperate and work with their pastor. The Lord gives them some visitation and insight and some harmony and obedience where they can be good workers with their pastors. They will have some imagination, and they can praise what the Lord has completed in their lives They take that and say, "Well, the Lord will call me to preach I have risen above this I see more than what I understand." Now they understand what they're doing. They understand their pastor. They understand their works. They understand the people. They love their pastor. They love what they're doing, but they looked and saw something else. They looked, and they looked too long and saw themselves elevated within their minds. They thought they should be equal with the pastor, equal with anyone, or the highest degree that God has handed down to man. Many of them give up the opportunity to do great works being the pastor's helper because of their imagination. They declare that the Lord has called them to preach, and they become enemies to themselves, because if the Lord did not call them. If the Lord did not inspire and choose you, He's not going to give you anything to do. Then, you sit around and want the pastor to stop His works. You want your pastor to stop preaching and let you do the preaching. And if that doesn't happen, you get angry and find fault in him. You cause conflict in the congregation and disrupt the whole church just because you looked too long. You saw too much that was not there. You saw yourself someplace where you shouldn't be in the first place. You saw yourself rising too fast. You saw yourself taking it for granted that you were good enough to be anything you wanted with God. But we need to learn the easy way—God gives us what He wants us to have. God uses us according to His own will. When we get tired of appreciating the way God uses us, we want to do it ourselves, and we change our entire life.

Sometimes we change from a good, innocent man to a mean man. A man who is in peace and enjoying life by serving becomes angry, disgusted, and trouble-minded. We drive ourselves away from God, away from people, and away from ourselves just because we looked too long. We didn't hear very much.

These brothers were helped, and they were blessed to be called and reminded. "Why are you standing there gazing up? You saw His power, His miracle. He just rose up, and all the clouds came down, and He just sat on them. They just rose up and carried Him easily out of your sight. And you are standing here looking, gazing. You have all your mind, your consciousness, your strength, your concentration, and your hope—all of that coming together while you look. If you look long enough, you'll become empty, drunk in your own imagination. You'll become helpless because you'll lose every hope, every practice, everything you have ever known. Every goal you have ever set, you're going to lose by just looking. You can always look Yes, you can always look. If you look long enough and let your imagination start forming desires, it takes you in. It's very dangerous. It is like the animals. It's very difficult to keep the cattle in their pastures if the grass in the adjoining pastures looks greener on the other side. Many times there is disappointment, because when they break the fence for the greener grass, they get there and find astroturf. That's very disappointing. We can't trust our eyes.

Our eyes are limited to truth. That way it's so good to have faith and patience and to be willing to be instructed by somebody. We can establish a life that is unlivable by deciding it by just looking. Many times we condemn ourselves by looking too long. We look too long in the wrong direction. We look for something that is not there. When our minds start playing tricks on us, we will almost be convinced that we have seen that for which we were looking. These brethren followed instructions, and they were unable to establish themselves out there on Mt. Olive with their divine imagination, some kind of false idea, or religious establishment.

That's why you have so many different kinds of beliefs, so many different kinds of faith floating around throughout the countries in our world today, simply because people see what they thought they saw. With young ministers, today it's frightening, because they come in, and they see everything. They see the Church after two thousand years. Everything about it is wrong. The minister is wrong. Their parents are wrong. The world is wrong. Can you imagine? They have all the answers, and the question is, from where did they get them?.

It doesn't matter who you are, if you don't know the situation, the inside and outside about anything, it's right with you, because you don't know the difference between right and the wrong.

This was the moving advice. A short message was given to His disciples that kept them from establishing or killing time out there and kept them from making a monument where Jesus was taken up.

I remember some time ago, when I made a visit to Jerusalem and other places over there. I had people try and show us the spot where Jesus was standing when He was taken up and where other people were standing and gazing up. Try to imagine what it was like saying, "If I had been here to look up." That came into my mind, and I said to myself, "I'm glad that I wasn't there, since I know what can happen to the mind of an individual." I probably wouldn't be as steadfast in the world today if I hadn't experienced the danger of imagination and building ideas, hopes, and testimonies on just what you see. All those who were looking with me that day couldn't help but think about when this took place, when Jesus was taken up. This was a kind of force, and I thought about this. This was the kind of force that confronted these brethren, because nobody knows how they really felt but them. They were there, but we know that there is less happening that can attract us.

People nowadays can be attracted by anything. Church people will leave their worship services because they are attracted by the sports world, ball games, fights, anything. You have choir members who will leave the choir stand in the middle of service, because they paid good money for tickets to go to some sporting event. Anything will attract most people, and they will walk away from their commitment to God. And to them, they are doing no wrong. Some say, "This is not Sunday. This is a week day, and I will go to church on Sunday." We can always justify ourselves, and this is why we are spiritually cold now. We can justify ourselves and feel good about it. We assume this is the way God sees it. We don't act according to the Word of God. We decide on what we think God should accept. We think when we do the things we do, we're doing it for God.

You're not doing the spiritual works of life for God. You're doing it as obedience unto God for yourself, because that is the promise. You work the works of faith, the works of salvation by faith, and He will give you eternal life. You're not doing God a favor. You're not doing the pastor a favor. You're doing yourself good, because you know this life is not a life in which you want to spend eternity. The Lord is offering you works that you can overcome.

I'm glad today. I'm glad for these angels. I'm glad the Lord sent these angels and sent them immediately, because it attracted them. It was at the moment, because He (Jesus) had just spoken. He just had said unto them, "You shall receive power, and after, the Holy Ghost shall come upon you." And He said, "You should be my witnesses." He also said now that their witnessing would begin, they would witness of Him at Jerusalem, Judaea, Samaria, and unto the uttermost part of the earth. That means that some kind of overwhelming religious idea establishment would have interrupted this great work of redemption that had been assigned to them.

At the time, these brethren—yes, he had smiled on them. He had told them to be filled with the Holy Ghost. How long would this last without power. They had the Holy Ghost, according to St. John 20. They had the Holy Ghost, but they didn't have the power. You see, if you are powerless, everything about you becomes helpless and lifeless. So, they had to have power before they could witness anywhere. This was in good time.

Don't stand there gazing up, go do what He said. If you do that, you can be His witnesses throughout the world, and that's what we are to do. Instead of looking, do it. Do what He says, and believe in doing. It depends on our accomplishments in life. By obeying, the power and the Gospel of Jesus Christ came. Then they obeyed the angels of the Lord, and they returned unto Jerusalem from the mountain that is called Mt. Olive. They continued in the Lord, and they accomplished what was promised. We have the same promises, but we'll have to stop looking and start doing. We'll have to believe in what we're doing and do what the Gospel has instructed us to do throughout the world and throughout our lives. God will bless and reward all according to His promises. Amen, Amen.

The Upper Room Experience

"And when they were come in, they went into an upper room, where abode both Peter, and James, and John, and Andrew, Philip, and Thomas, Bartholomew, and Matthew, James the son of Alphaeus, and Simon Zelotes, and Judas the brother of James." (Acts 1:13)

And when they were come in, they went up into an upper room where they abode. As the disciples had returned from Jerusalem, from their great adventure on Mt. Olivet where they saw Jesus ascend unto Heaven, they came back to Jerusalem. The distance was a Sabbath day's journey. This measurement was the biblical analysis of the distance from Mt. Olivet to Jerusalem. But they were very serious about their return to the city. As the text tells us, they went directly to the upper room, the place where they were to wait for the promises. And it goes further and says that they were of one accord. It was no problem for them to all be together and arrive at the same place together. This is what one accord will do for you. It will bring you together, and you have no problem walking, talking, conducting yourselves together with one thing in mind.

As they were at this place, let us note some additions that we don't have in the text, and how the additions come about. There were more to the numbers who received this commission from Christ, because in this counsel with Jesus and their final meeting with Him, when He ascended, He went unto Heaven and instructed them to go to the upper room. Arriving at the upper room, the number had increased, and that gives us to understand that there had been some increase in the knowledge of the works that took place in the minds of the disciples. This increase opened the door for others to be a part of that ministry, because when they had settled, the number had risen from eleven to around one hundred and twenty. Peter and the others had shown where they had been searching the Scriptures of the prophesy about the time, this time, that would come. It led them to open to women and other brethren, which added to the original number. There had to be some concern about the time it was taking for the promises to arrive. It may not seem like it, but to be housed in and prayerfully wait for ten days is a mighty long time

In this period, we discover that Peter began to stand up and act like a leader. When he stood up among the others, he began to call their attention to the situation he had discovered concerning their wait. No doubt, recognizing the time that was wasting, and knowing his Lord wouldn't have taken that long to arrive in Heaven and send the power on them, Peter, through his evaluation, realized that there could have been something that may have caused the delay. As we look, Acts 1:15 says, "And in those days Peter stood up in the midst of the disciples, and said, (the number of names together were about an hundred and twenty)...." And his concern was that there was something that was causing a delay, and it has to be among them. He discovered that the power couldn't come until they were completely organized, suitable with the scripture. He said in Acts1:16, "Men and brethren, the scripture needs have been fulfilled, which the Holy Ghost by the mouth of David spake before concerning Judas which was a guide to them that took Jesus, and we have a vacancy, not suitable to the prophets for the works of the Lord. He concluded they must offer this situation before the Lord so the vacancy could be fulfilled and the words of the prophets could also be fulfilled. He began to talk about the harmony and the kind of individual it would take to insert into this vacancy on the board. He began to remember those who were in their presence and in the presence of Jesus in the period of John the Baptist until the day that the Lord was taken up. They began to realize the names, and came to a selection of two. Peter began to perform as an individual who was filled with the Holy Ghost, and he began to act differently than he had in the past with a hot temper. Peter was known for his temper, for his speaking out of order, and for blasting. But he began to demonstrate that a change was taking place. He was able to stand, not as he had in the past as an individual, speaking for himself, by himself, not expecting to be witnessed by anyone. Peter spoke as a leader, and he expected the witnessing to come from those that were with him. He went far enough to give the details of Judas's desire. He chose to take the exit of life his own way, and he went down the wrong road by choice and action. He talked about the disaster and the dead end of his life as well as the suffering that Judas chose for himself.

That is an example for all of us. Life depends upon the choices you make. In this salvation, in this justification, the Lord did not place a command that we command to be saved or we command to repent, but He left it as a choice, and we choose to be what we want at the present time or in the future, in this life or the life to come.

We don't try to force men to repent, we encourage them and try to help them see and understand the reason that they should repent. I think when we demonstrate to them that we have a choice to make and explain to them the difference in making the choice, to accept Christ in their lives or to remain without Him. we need to be mindful of how we pressure and drive those individuals. It's very difficult for us to make up our minds about something we have never experienced. You have to do it yourself, and all by yourself. We cannot make up their minds for them. We cannot confess for them. We cannot repent for them, but we can counsel with them, offer some insight on life, and give them some uncertainty about life. But they have to make up their own minds.

So, Peter said, Judas chose to break away. He chose to take that step in life. I believe before you even change in life to go to something else, you need to evaluate where you are and who you are at the present time. It seems that Judas was different. He had different ideas. He was thinking about some of the same ideas that some of his brethren were thinking. They were thinking as the rest that Jesus would set up an earthly kingdom, that He would reign as king on the throne. But the difference was the rest were humble. They listened and followed Jesus They waited for Him to give them the truth about His Kingdom. In the last visit, as we mentioned previously, they spoke to the point. They were sure He was going to do it, but they wanted to know, "Are you going to restore it back to Israel now, or when?" Of course you have the answer to that, but Judas pressed the issue. He knew that Jesus had great miracles and power beyond mankind. He had experienced being with Him. He obeyed Him. He experienced how the wind and all powers obeyed His voice, and Judas felt if He had forced the issue, on behalf of Christ's enemy, Jesus would strike back or defeat them in their efforts to challenge them.

According to Judas's testimony which we read about, he was very disappointed and let down when he saw that Jesus wasn't violent and didn't lose his temper when He was arrested; instead, he humbled Himself and commanded Peter to do the same. By putting away His sword, Jesus was not going to raise His voice or defeat the force for the purpose of those who came to take Him. Something else we discovered about Judas was that he wasn't paying attention to what Jesus was saying, because Jesus told them many times that He would give Himself over to the hands of wicked sinners and that they would crucify Him. And even when it came to the hour, Jesus spoke, even at the last supper. He talked about the disaster of the man who would betray Him. One of the writers said it would be better if that man would have been born dead. I think we should recognize the greatest and the wisest opportunity we have is to make the choice concerning our eternity. We will receive it and or come to our destiny by the choice that we make now. Our choice is what will separate us, the saints, from the sinners, depending upon what we choose now. We choose the road we travel, the decisions we make, and the life that we take on in this life that leads us to eternal life. Peter remembered these things, and he saw, prayerfully. The Scripture tells us they were waiting in prayer, because they had no doubt that their Lord would deliver.

Peter explained to those who were there that they must fill the vacancy. As they selected two, they didn't take the chance of making the choice themselves. They didn't try to decide who was qualified or who would be the best person to fill Judas's space. They selected two, Barsabas (surname Justus) and Matthias. They brought them before the Lord and prayed that the Lord would choose one of the two men to fill the space. The biblical terms they used in those days were for them to cast lots, and they cast lots expecting the Lord to direct them. He did, and it fell on Matthias. They were happy the Lord had made a choice from the two to make this number, to fill the space that was standing before the arrival of the Holy Ghost, the promise of God.

I think it is easy for us to take a note because we have the same privileges. We have the same incidents throughout our lives, and we have to make similar decisions concerning our lives.

I think it should disturb us when we have problems in our prayers in making a connection or when we find our spirit begin to get low, and slip away and when we lose our spiritual consciousness. We find ourselves failing to have the increase of spiritual momentum. We should know how to examine ourselves and know the problem for one thing. Peter understood that the problem was not in the Lord. Something was out of place with them and in their lives, and when he discovered it, he called together the followers who were with him. They handled it beautifully, preparing themselves for the greatest adventure life would ever know. They had no way to understand that for which they were waiting. The words of promise were good enough for them. They had conceded that the Lord Jesus would always deliver. So, they waited. What were they waiting for? They were waiting for the promise that Jesus said, "Ye shall receive power after the Holy Ghost has come upon you." Your life will take a turn for the best. You will no longer be my followers, but you will be my witnesses.

We discover this in our churches. We have many people, people who confess that Jesus is in their lives, but they refuse to be the kind of followers the Holy Spirit causes people to be. You discover that most people want to have their way want everything their way. Many challenge their leaders and exchange words and ideas with their own pastors. You wonder about those kind of people. You wonder about them. You wonder if they will ever understand that if you cannot follow, you will never be able to witness. You learn by following.

We remind them they are to be disciples of Christ. That's something about which we never remind them—what Christ requires of His leaders, His ministers, and His missionaries. They are to make disciples for Him. He didn't say member. He didn't say people, or groups, or families. He said, make disciples unto me. Being a disciple means following Jesus. We don't ever remind them that they must become disciples. If you want to call yourself a member, go ahead and call yourself a member, but be a disciple, because if you are not a disciple and following Jesus, you won't ever be a missionary to witness for Him. When we are followers of Him, we are learning, and when we are witnessing, we are laboring for Him. These go together. That's why we are the Church, because the Church emerges and brings us together. The Church functions depends upon how well it does.

Now, it's no problem to discover when people haven't really accepted Christ, because we understand the works of the Church. The Church is a mission. The Church is the mission, that's what it is, a mission that was born and built the way the Lord builds. The Lord builds with livelihood. The carpenters build with hammers, nails, and mortar and bricks, but Jesus builds with life. Whatever Jesus builds is alive. Therefore the material with which he builds, is the ingredient of himself. His Kingdom is made up within Him. He is the foundation. We build upon that foundation. When we accept Christ, we have the means, what it takes to build upon that foundation. That's why the Church was born. It was born with the requirement of serving God and building His Kingdom.

The church, the New Testament Church, the only Church, is a preaching church. It's a witnessing church. It's a praying church. It's a fellowshipping church. It's a testifying church. It's a compassionate church. All of these things is of what the mission is made, which is the Church. These are the things that are performed in our lives. Of course, we call it the Holy Spirit, because the Holy Spirit is within the

Church and the life of the Church. But we're talking about the duty and the function of the Church, Jesus said it will guide you. It will keep you. It will preserve you. It will teach you all things. It will teach you things about me, things about me that I haven't taught you. Jesus referred to Him as the other comforter, and the other comforter, who is riding on the inside, directs us.

Many people who try to single out the human spirit of God don't seem to think that the Spirit is only designed to make you happy. But the Spirit becomes the motivation of your life. He directs us, wherever—on our jobs and on the byways of life. Wherever you are, He's there, controlling, cautioning you, and directing you on how to conduct yourself. He is on your job directing you how to be honest and true to your job and to the employees. He teaches you to give an honest day's work and to be truthful to those with whom you work. He teaches you to tell the truth and to be truthful in all things. He directs us to respect and to appreciate one another, to see men as men, as human beings. He seeks for that one good thing in every individual. Every individual who has life has a portion of God. God is life. God is in nothing that has no life. God is alive, and nothing dead whatsoever can be found in God. So it doesn't matter how cruel a man is, or how many wrongdoings an individual has committed, if he still lives, he still has that good part. God's in him.

That's why I couldn't serve on grand jury or be on a jury to condemn or to vote on capital punishment for someone even if I wanted to. The office that I hold, I believe, won't allow me to do so. To vote to tamper with that small portion of life which keeps every human being alive, that's God. Never could I vote for that to be taken by anyone else but God Himself.

The Church won't ever die. The Church is life; there's no death in the church. That's why Jesus is coming to receive His Church. That's what He promised to come back and receive, His Church and those who have accepted Him. When He comes, there will be a completion to His Kingdom, which He built in our hearts. If you don't have that Kingdom in your heart, if you don't exist with the Church working and its mission carrying on, it's woe unto you when Jesus comes. So, you cannot be in that Church. That Church will have to be in you. There are many people who have left congregations, and places and feel as if they have joined many churches. That's sad. You cannot join the church. The Church was born, and the Church has to be built in you through birth and with the handwork of Jesus Christ.

That's the problem with our unspiritual worship and our weak and unproductive worship. We are in the Church, and the Church is not in us. When the world gets in the Church, if the world can get in the Church, it will no longer be the Church. The church is in the world, but not of the world. Most people we have active in our congregation are people of the world, unconverted people, unspiritual people, people who are not born of the Lord Jesus Christ, and people who were not born of the Holy Spirit. These are the kinds of people who are eyeing the organization, which we misunderstand to be the Church. We're hoping, in our coming outline, to be able to explain to you the birth of the Church. This will help you to understand that the Church is not an organization but an organism.

Amen, Amen.

The Birth of the Church

"And when the day of Pentecost was fully come, they were all with one accord in one place. And suddenly there came a sound from heaven as of a rushing mighty wind, and it filled all the house where they were sitting. And there appeared unto them cloven tongues like as of fire, and it sat upon each of them. And they were all filled with the Holy Ghost, and began to speak with other tongues, as the Spirit gave them utterance." (Acts 2: 1-4)

This is the most important chapter of the New Testament. The rest of them are giving information concerning the Church. The second chapter of Acts gives us the birth of the Church. Now, these are the promises; they have made their arrival. Those disciples along with the additional one hundred and twenty, were the ones to wait and to receive the establishment of the Kingdom of our Lord. It's no longer identified as the Kingdom, but as the Church. The New Testament, especially, is the history of the Church. The Letters of the New Testament are concerning the Church, the Church being born.

Let us notice what took place at the arrival of this great power, which has been talked about by the prophets and declared by Jesus Christ himself, who is the fulfillment of all the promises. Even the promises of the prophets were fulfilled through the ministry and the life of Jesus, through the Son of God, and the analysis of His sonship on earth. Jesus laid the foundation, and He called the personnel, He trained them and made them aware of this day that was coming. This was the purpose of the sonship of the Son of God, the sonship. The Son of God was the servant of God to minister this redemption on Earth. Jesus was not born in heaven; He was born on Earth. He came from Heaven, but He was born through the human portion. He had taken on the body of human, and it all was earthly. His name was Jesus; His other names of who He was and who He is came from Heaven.

His earthly name was here before He came. His name, Jesus, a common Greek name, was given by the prophet. He came into the world and took on that name. He served His sonship on Earth with the name Jesus. He invested and labored in that name with all pertaining to his present personality and existence. That name was noted to be the key to all things. That name disturbed and electrified and stirred up. Those who came to know that name were lifted up and rejoiced in that name Jesus. Some became offended and tried to destroy Him and that name. But when He finished the works that He came to do, and when He departed and returned back to His throne, returned back to His Lordship, His God and self-existence, He did not carry the name with Him. He left the name so His followers, His believers, His Church could always look to Him, pray to Him, come to Him, and believe in Him, all by that name. You can't do anything. You can't believe anything or ask anything without the name Jesus. The Bible declares the only way to be saved is by that name. The only way to approach God is by that name. He fulfilled and added to that earthly name and made it the heavenly key and a blessing to every person of all generations, and all nations who can praise God by that name. The Son of God was the image and power of God on Earth. But there are no works done on the sonship of God. Jesus came down and became the Son of God. The Son died because it had ended the mission that He came to do. The name was left to us. God made Him Lord and Christ. Lord means ownership. Jesus is Lord. Jesus is God. He's Lord God. He's Lord and Christ, and we approach Him by His name.

When He returned and ten days later, He came back in the power of the Holy Ghost. We try to make an extension between the two, but there is no way you can place a period or a comma between Jesus and the Holy Ghost, because they are one. They are one who came to the world together. The difference between Jesus being in the Holy Ghost and in His sonship is in sonship time. He was visible. He was visible and unlimited in power. Jesus had all power on Earth and no power could defeat His call on Earth. But when He approached Heaven, He prayed like any other person to His father to deliver to Him His needs from Heaven.

Some declare He wouldn't give up that portion of power in Heaven to come down and make the sacrifice, because that was pleasing to God, because that was God's good pleasure for Him to do so. He pleased God by dying and suffering. He pleased God so well, He was able to endure without even getting an answer to His prayer in the garden at Gethsemane.

He is the only one that you know, or read about, who is father and son, too. No one else could say that I am in the Father, and the Father is in me. The self-existence and ownership is beyond men's comprehension.

If you will notice, people are still calling Him to come and save them. Jesus died in our place and rose to our justification. He suffered one time. He died one time. He rose one time. He saved us, the world, one time. Every person, before and after, has already been saved, but they haven't all accepted. If you accept Christ in your life, I don't mean some thoughts about it; I mean believe on Him, accept Him, depend on Him in your life, He saves by His grace.

He's not my savior; He was my savior. He saved me, but He is my Lord. He's the Lord of my life. He's the Lord of your life, because He owns us. He bought us with a price. He paid the price with His own blood.

Let us notice that this Church has been born. As Jesus spoke openly and questioned concerning the Church in St. Matthew 16, He spoke and questioned His disciples and Peter concerning the Church. He made a promise by saying, "On this rock I will build my Church; and the gates of hell shall not prevail against it." And it goes on. When Peter had answered Jesus's question, "Whom do men say that I the son of man am?" Peter said, "Thou art the Christ." Jesus cautioned Peter then, saying that his remark did not come from him, because he was flesh and blood. That kind of answer comes not from flesh and blood at this time. But Peter, you have something that you never had. You have a revelation from Heaven, and God just revealed this answer, which was the truth unto you. Peter, because of this, on this rock I will build my Church. Not only that Peter, I will give unto you the keys to the Kingdom. Whatsoever you bind on Earth you shall bind in Heaven.

Let's notice that the Church was conceived at that time. Notice the quietness. When something is conceived, it is mostly quiet time. Peter was told by this revelation from Heaven and the true Word from God. Peter was not enthusiastic He didn't say a word. He didn't say, "Amen." He didn't say, "Praise God." He didn't say, "Hallelujah." He said not a word. He was quiet. Peter was unaware of what was happening. Giving him the key points to some authority, some action, some promotion of this Kingdom, but he still didn't say a word. But when the Church was born, it began as if they had been praying and waiting in one accord, and the time had fully come. It had come not late, not early, not accidentally, not partly, but fully. It came as a sound from Heaven, as a rushing mighty wind.

I think about the ownership and that everything is at the service of the almighty God. We talked earlier about how Jesus used the clouds to go up without any misfortune. Calmly and intelligently, they just carried Him to Heaven. He came back riding the wind, and the wind was heard, and the wind was not just breezy; it blew enough to have a sound, and the sound was from Heaven. When you think about it when did church people become so quiet? From where did they get all of this stillness? Their dryness? Their unspiritual attitude?

When the Church came and was born it was on its way. You see, the Church came from Heaven. Let's notice this. It came from Heaven. Jesus returned to Heaven within ten days in the power of the Holy Ghost. That same Jesus that you saw going up to Heaven, you'll see Him in the same like manner coming not only with the clouds, but with the company of the wind. Clouds don't make sound, but wind makes sounds. The sound was from Heaven, and this wind had a force, because in Acts 2, verse two, it says, "There came a sound from Heaven as of a rushing mighty wind." It came in a hurry, because it came on time. It came with force, because it had a mighty job to do. It delivered so much. It delivered the Kingdom that Jesus had built through His ministry and life and which he carried to Heaven and established in His own power.

Note this action and work from visible to invisible. He took control of the wind and all of its resources and came down to mankind. He brought His Kingdom down. It was a rushing, mighty wind. It filled all the house where they were sitting.

Now that's what happens when God comes in, regardless of where. He's in all places. He said I'm present. He's everywhere. He does not come or He does not go. He's everywhere at the same time. So He fills up. And when He comes into the life of an individual, He fills it up because He establishes His Kingdom in the lives of every believer who receives Him and accepts Him. He fills us up. I wonder how we could confess that He has entered into our lives, and we have so much emptiness, so much vacancy, so much time to do everything but to respond to the works of the Kingdom.

Most people play the works of the Church half time. Some have only certain Sunday mornings; some are Sunday morning specialists. Some go only on Sunday morning. Regardless of what other services you have, they will not show up. There are those, also, who have certain days that they make themselves present, all to identify something that does not exist. You cannot represent, you cannot be the Church unless the Church has been established in your life, in your heart. You don't have to go around with a tag, chain, r cross, or sign to tell people what you are. At every function, you are identified by your work. By your acts, your personality , your labor, your company, your presence, you reveal what's inside, the function of the Church. You don't have to use anything else to broadcast who and what you are.

So the house was filled when they were sitting. Now what happens here? If the Spirit filled the house, then the Spirit wrapped up and entered every soul, every person who was in the house. When it filled the sets, it filled their hearts and their minds. It filled everything about them, meaning He had received them and taken them in. But when all of this happened, the Spirit, the wind, came in and filled their hearts and the place, and it filled up everything. It united and sealed that one accord that cannot be broken by anything. That given fellowship of the Church cannot be broken. Isn't it strange that people spend their lives leaping and jumping from one congregation to another, one title to another, and one place to another and feel good about it? They feel as if they are better than their condition. But theirs was a fellowship that cannot be broken, which unites us together and holds us together as it held those who were waiting to receive the Church.

When all of this had taken place, something began to happen, according to that third verse. Something different started appearing unto them, cloven tongues like as of fire. If you notice the word cloven, you will find that it has a special power that acts and establishes special ingredients in this work. It fills man with a special power that works and performs as if it never happened in mankind. It dealt with their tongues and with their minds. It went through them and brought about a healing—a healing of their wounds, a healing of distress, a healing of sinners. It was a long for the arrival of this power. It says, "And there it appeared unto them cloven tongues like as of fire." It was like the fire that was mentioned in the works and the cleansing. It means it's not like the physical fire with its only purpose being to burn. It burns, and when it burns you purify. When fire burns, it purifies. You purify water with physical fire. It's hot; it burns. You can also weaken things. Men can take fire and heat steel and iron to shape it any way they want to, because the fire comes with strength. It controls. It has the strength to remold or to remake. This fire burns away the kind of effectiveness that is essential to our life of purity. He forgives the sins, and burns away the scars the sins have made—wrong desires and wrong thoughts. It purifies. It cleans your mind and removes all these things. It burns away the human Adam, the old Adam man, that appetite that causes you to go after and turn from the principles of God. All of that vanishes. That fire cleans it up.

Can you imagine that fire sitting upon each of them? When this happened, when it sat upon them, it had the control to find every complaint and every bit of scar tissue that had scarred them. It purified and healed the wound that sin had made in our lives.

Those whom it touched, how long did it take to touch? How long did it take to burn when it purified and removed these things from us. Verse four says, "And they were all filled with the Holy Ghost, and began to speak with other tongues, as the Spirit gave them utterance." Now when they were filled with the Holy Spirit, they couldn't keep silent. They had to speak, because they were caught up in these special powers, these cloven tongues. And they were able to speak, and they were not speaking of themselves because of these new experiences. They were filled, and as the Spirit was taking them in, and filling them with the Kingdom of God, which is the Church and all it replaced, every step, every custom, every self-made plan was replaced. Their occupations, their motives, and their destiny, all of these things came through a change. The foundation of their lives had been built upon the foundation that Jesus laid. They became qualified and ready to carry on according to His word.

So this is where the Kingdom was established and began to be built. And this Kingdom, which is the Church is not completed yet. It will not be completed until the Church has delivered the word of God and the Gospel has been preached by the Church unto all the world.

Somebody will question the Church how will preach. The Church has its preachers. We are the Church. We are the spokesmen for the Church. The minister is the overseer, the captain of the ship. He is the one with the oversight and the vision to keep his followers and his co-workers going in the right direction. He has the responsibility to feed them. He's obligated to feed the flock. Jesus said He bought it, and He requires us to feed it. He bought it through birth. He established it. It is born, and we are to feed it.

When we are preaching the Word, we are preaching the Church. Isn't it strange that we have people in many departments of the Church who participate in everything, musicals and every kind of program, and they care nothing about preaching? If anything is left out of their life and plans, it is preaching. How can you fail to receive the Gospel when that is the food already prepared to feed you? How are you going to have strength to grow when you are not fed with the Gospel of Jesus Christ?

I tell you, and I have mentioned it before, our performance in our worship services is a formality. Many times those who listen to us cannot listen to the seriousness that should be there. There's always some kind of human display of spiritual entertainment when this Church has the power of the Holy Spirit and the function of the Kingdom of God to seek the lost. Without the lost, or the seeking for the lost, we are not doing the will of the Lord.

This is an outreach Church. We are seeking those who don't know Christ. There's room enough, and each time a soul repents and comes to Christ the Kingdom is being built. Sooner or later, it's going to be complete, and Jesus will appear. I like the way the Apostle Paul said when He appears we will all be like Him. You can't get in this Church; the church must be in you. You can get in Christ, but not the Church. The Church has to be in you.

Amen, Amen.

The Church Moves from the House

"And there were dwelling at Jerusalem Jews, devout men, out of every nation under Heaven. Now when this was noised abroad, the multitude came together, and were confounded, because that every man heard them speak in his own language. And they were all amazed and marveled, saying one to another, Behold are not all these which speak Galilaeans? And how hear we every man in our own tongue, wherein we were born?" (Acts 2:5-8)

As we have mentioned in the previous messages about the Church being born in the upper room, I think it is important for us to recognize that the Church was born inside, in the house. But it didn't remain in the house after all the spiritual impact that has been declared at the birth of the Church. They immediately had to move from the house, because the dimension of the Church swiftly outgrew the house. The second point is, those who were present (the one hundred and twenty) were waiting for the promises to come. The power of the Holy Spirit overshadowed all. The Kingdom of God was established with all the one hundred and twenty, and there was no need for them to remain in the house, because their work and their world was on the outside. It's easy to understand according to the entire passage of Scripture that we have before us. The text says all nations, men of all nations under the Heaven, were waiting on the outside.

This explains that in our works of salvation and our outreach of evangelism, we spend too much time on the inside and do not carry on our work of evangelism to the outside. So, it is the mission of the Church to not dwell and spend all this time in the house. The harvest and the work is on the outside. It would have been fruitless for this one hundred and twenty to remain in the upper room discussing the joy of the Holy Spirit that they had experienced. That would have been nonproductive. Their mission required them to face an unborn world as they began fulfilling the promises that Jesus said earlier, that when this happens, ye shall be witnesses unto me. The beginning at Jerusalem was urgent for them to begin then and there. Thank God this is what happened. When they had gone through the change and been well-equipped with all the necessities to go out and make known that Jesus was alive and had returned to speak unto them and to receive them unto Himself as Lord and Christ, they began to come in unity together to meet the nations on the outside.

Again, there's nothing to accomplish on the inside. There's no fruit to gather to keep rehearsing the same thing over and over to those who are supposed to be witnessing to the unsaved. The power and the unity bought them from the house unto the open world where there were many who had not yet experienced or who were aware of what was going on.

There were some hoping to join in and be a part of this great event. There were some who were blind and were criticizing their emotional act and their mysterious speaking and attitude. And we noticed there were cries made from those on the outside saying, "Sir, what must we do that we might be a part of this?" Peter gladly proclaimed in his introduction that they needed to put first things first, and that is to repent, believe, and be baptized in the name of the Lord Jesus Christ, and they would be saved. In that kind of invitation, the Word extended the numbers rapidly and they grew fast. That means they were in the right direction. Just think, it would have been impossible for this to take place in the house. For many of our leaders today, pride will not let them walk out of the pulpit and go on the outside of the house. They have made their world in the house, and they feel everything, according to their minister's ability, is to be performed in the house. Well, how can you add? How can you prepare the people for the Lord to add to the Church when the addition is on the outside? They don't hear, they don't see, and there is very little that attracts, because those who are on the inside of the house have very little information when they come from the house because the works and the responsibility of our people seems to be that they are responsible to serve in the house and have no responsibilities when they leave the house. So, it is urgent that we might understand that the house of God is built for the Church to move in and praise God, give thanks to God, and move out of the house and serve the Lord.

Through the service made on the outside, the outreach and the possibilities of increasing the number of witnesses was greater. This was a time when the disciples had the privilege to fulfill the instruction of Jesus when He said, "Go and make disciples unto me." The purpose of making disciples is that you will have to go out where men are not disciples, which means followers of Christ. Until we change our shoes, change our minds, change our programs, and move out of the house, we will never be able to win disciples unto Christ.

People hardly hear the words of the disciples. Now people are known as *added members* of the Church. Well, who ever added members to the Church? They didn't add the biblical responsibilities that are required for discipleship, which means to do the whole will of our Lord Jesus. To do that, we must be born so that the Church is established in our hearts and becomes our lives. One thing, we must understand, has blocked our knowledge in recognizing that the Church is alive in us. It's because Jesus said, "I will build my Church." One thing we must understand, when man thinks of building, he thinks of the materialistic world and how he builds. We build with material—saws, hammers, mortar, and bricks. We gather material to build. But the Lord builds, and whatever the Lord builds is life. Whatever the Lord builds consists of life. His Kingdom was built with life in life, and He expects it to continue to be built in your life. You cannot be a portion of this Kingdom building without giving your life to be built. Life extends from one to the other, because every time someone comes and accepts Jesus Christ and is filled with the Holy Spirit, it adds to the addition of the building of the Kingdom of our Lord.

We understand that the Kingdom of God, which Jesus built, is the Church. And it's known by the name Church because it's an earthly operation; it's an earthly establishment. But, the Church is the Kingdom of the Lord that's being built through the Church. And when the Kingdom is complete, then Jesus will come. Until we recognize that the kingdom of Israel was replaced by the building of the Church, we will never be able to find ourselves in our rightful place to let our lives be the works of the Church.

Now, these brethren had to move out of the house because their lives had become this great mission of the Kingdom of God, which is the Church. It had to move, because it possessed every ingredient that it required for the Church to make it known in the hearts of men and women in the world and to bring them unto Christ through the power of the Holy Spirit. What is this Church that was born? What is this Church that moves from the house? Well, it moves at work. It's a preaching Church. It's a praying church. It's a testifying Church. It's a compassionate church. It's an outreach church. It's a faithful church. It's a church of hope. It's a church that never stops. It's a church that lights up. It's a city that sits on the hill and cannot be hidden. It's a church that doesn't live on the outside of the individual. It's a church that human beings cannot enter. It's a Church that human beings cannot control. It's a Church with it's own decisions.

It's a Church that has all its rules and regulations. You don't rule the Church. You don't motivate the Church. You're not in the Church; the Church is in you. The Church has the life of motivation. The Church has the life of spiritual advantage. The Church has the life of Christ, because the body of Christ is the Church. The spirit of Christ is the life of the Church. The Church holds the promises that Jesus will come and possess the Church when the time comes and the Kingdom has been completed. Then He will come and call the order for His assessment to judge the world. Therefore, your labor is out of the house. We are calling upon every believer, who thinks he or she is a believer, and who desire to be a believer, to remember Jesus explains this in His early ministry by saying, "Except a man be born again, he cannot see the kingdom of God." (John 3:3) So, you have to be born first so the Church can be established in you. When you are born of the Holy Spirit, the Holy Spirit and the power of the Church comes in the same package. You cannot be a representative unless you are born again. When you are born again, you have begun with new power and new control. You're in a new world with new activities. You have a new mind. You have a new outlook, and you have a new destiny where we are all traveling in the same direction.

Oh, if we would only wake up and move out of these organizations that we call Church, where we spend our time going in the name of the Church. Men and women are living and dying not knowing what the Church really is or of what it consists. Organizations have drained all of the notions from people's minds. They have caused congregations to become ice cold, dumb, unable to sing, unable to witness, and unable to stay awake. Sitting in church on Sunday morning, our notion of entertainment is the choir singing, clapping, clowning, and making up their own spiritual involvements and feeling as if they have accomplished something, but when they walk out of the choir stand, they are no better off than they were before. It's time for us to preach the sound doctrine of Jesus Christ, and be steadfast in the Apostolic doctrine, which is the doctrine of Jesus Christ.

Our world has become blind and staggering. Everything is happening, and it seems as if it is getting worse. God's purpose and plan is blocked by human organization and human plans.

Many ministers are pastoring churches today, and they don't even know if it has a discipline or not. They don't worry about their programs. They set it by making calendars for monthly reminders or whatever. God has nothing to do with their programs, because God doesn't make programs twelve months in advance. It's not that kind of operation.

We must stop our fancy way of doing. We must realize there is something seriously wrong. Most people who commit some terrible crime have their names on some congregation's role. If that is not enough to remind us that something is wrong, I would like to know what other steps can you take. Just follow the New Testament Church. Just obey the doctrine of it, and we will maintain the power of the kind of men who preach and have some affect on the communities wherever you go. You must begin to proclaim and labor from the outside.

Now, when the echoes of the Church had moved from the house, it was noticed by the noise that came from the multitude, and those who listened in were confounded. They discovered something that had never been before. Every man who heard them speak in his own tongue could understand. That was the miracle in the language and voices of the apostles and witnesses, who met with the understanding of every man who heard them. It was something, because it was something that had never been known in the world before. They were amazed and they marveled to themselves, one to another, by saying, "Behold, are not all these which speak Galilaeans?" They began to express their opinions, and some were moved with desires to be a part of this great event.

Now, instead of understanding how the Church was born and how it exploded in the minds of those who were blessed to be the individuals, we have proof of it, and with our own conclusions, we tried to build on it. But there is, according to our scriptures, no other foundation except the one that has been laid. No one can build on that foundation except the one who builds the foundation, and that is Jesus Christ Himself.

They were amazed and questioned, "How hear we every man in our own tongue, wherein we were born?" The same tongue with which they were born they could speak and give us understanding, and no one could say, "I don't understand." The power of the message and the Holy Spirit had made known to them that what they saw and what was going on was that the Kingdom was being built, and the door was open to everyone who wanted to repent, deny himself, come, and be a part of this great event.

There is something else that we need to think about. This was an unusual time in Jerusalem. Usually when there is some great crowd or some noisy event, you'll immediately experience having the police force there, or the Roman solders would have rushed in and tried to put down the disturbance. But isn't it beautiful at this time you didn't hear of the police force? Where was the police force? Where were the soldiers? Where was that force that had been a stumbling block to keep this power from spreading for the last three years? See how at this period, at this time, they were all swept under the rug. Now, everything was in one accord, and all was emerging in the same happening. It was a time, a glorious time. It was a time when men tried to figure out or tried to imagine what it was like, because it had never happened before. How many nations had been steadfast in their own gods, in their own religion, and would not listen or pay attention to what was said in Jesus's preaching or His teaching? Many were coming, joining in, seeking the way, seeking the Word, seeking and saying, "What can I do to be a part of this?"

It's wonderful how this one hundred and twenty grew in such a short time. As it grew, power and the works became more real and more powerful. They didn't forget to carry on their daily responsibility, to recognize their physical needs. They made provision for food to eat and for food for those who didn't have food and shelters, because they had all things common. They were in one accord. No one was trying to just think of himself or do for himself. They were willing and ready to share. Their minds and their hearts were open and their lives were experiencing a great change, and a great outlook, when they didn't look on men as Hebrews, or Greeks, or Gentiles. They saw all men as brethren, as men who loved one another, who had compassion for one another, and who were willing to share with one another.

These are the functions of the Church. When we find ourselves on the outside not caring about people and their affairs and how they are getting along, their haves and their have-nots, when this becomes none of our concern, then that's telling us that we are losing, have lost, or have never known the mission of the Church.

Well, what is this Church? Let's talk a little about the substance of this Church. This Church is the guide. It's the preserver. It's the keeper. This Church goes where we go. It makes our home on the level of the Church everywhere. It makes us no longer one thing at the house of God and something else at our house. Our house becomes a place where it is ready for right things and right people to come together and have a fruitful conversation, the ways and means to help and protect each other's reputation and each other's weakness, to help with each other's children, and to make sure, even in our home, that it's known that the Lord dwells in this place. I don't think we will feel comfortable, even in our own home, if we are practicing things that are not unacceptable to the Holy Spirit. We should not practice all kinds of entertainment, all kinds of drinks, all kinds of games, and all kinds of music. What comes from our homes should place a bitter taste in the mouths of those who are ungodly. But this Church will make it known that any home identified as this city that sits on a hill always has something to be offered. You can get conversation. You can get counsel. You can get help and advice. You can get strength in prayers. You can get comfort in the experience. You can get hope from the Church's expression in its belief. All of these things you can receive in the homes where the Church lives or the Church dwells. The message which criticizes, is low rating, and destroys other's characters is not exercised in the home where the Church lives. Unspiritual music and loud, unnecessary noise and language that comes from most of our homes would not be discovered in the homes where the Church dwells.

Even on the job, we should be honest, fair, and true to the employers, making sure that they get a full day's work for the pay that we get, a day of honest work. They shouldn't have to worry about things being misplaced or taken because the Church is on the job. The places where you dwell can always attract those who are not familiar with kindness, good conversation, or an intelligent personality who is filled with respect and gratitude and is willing to share the best with the neighbors. This is the main work of the Church.

Something else this Church consists of is every believer. Everyone who is a part of this Church is the mission, and that mission is the entire Church. This Church's mission consists of preaching, teaching, and evangelism. It is the home of responsibility, which is known as a home mission and a foreign mission. It is responsible for Christian training, a one-on-one outreach, and seeking lost souls. And for its life, it relies on the Holy Spirit for strength. It has the spirit of fellowship. It has a tendency to love and sees all men as human beings and all men as brothers. It consists of all of thing so that what you automatically consist of when you are born of the Holy Spirit and this Kingdom is established in you consists of that. And the only thing you should do is pray that you be strengthened in all of these works, because you are that, and you must be strong and able to carry it out.

It's strange how we spend our time. People have been in congregations all their lives, and you are still trying to train them to do just certain things. We are this already. You need to pray and seek the Lord that He might strengthen you and guide you to do what you are supposed to do. You are supposed to follow the directions of the Church that lives in you. When you hear the Word preached, it revives. This is what happens to people of the Church. When you hear the Gospel preached, it revives you to witness the importance of your mission, what you are responsible to do. It answers questions that you don't understand about what you are supposed to do. That is why it's so important for you to hear the Gospel so that you can continue to grow in strength. Now strength doesn't automatically come.

Just because you are born again and that the Church has been built in you doesn't mean for you to stop and not pray, and to not receive instructions from those who are able to do so—the minister, the teachers, or whomever. When you hear this, it falls into place. because that's in you, and this helps to bring out the works and activity that you have in you already. Many people have the Church in them, and they don't know it. They don't know it. The pastor has to put his finger on everything or say everything to get them to do, and they have it already in them. The only thing you have to do is pray and put forth an effort. Practice, and it will automatically work in you. So remember that the Church moved out of the house, and no house has ever been able to house it and never will. It is too great to be shut in. Amen, Amen.

Church Works and the Works of the Church: There's a Difference Between Church Work and the Works of the Church

"And they, continuing daily with one accord in the temple, and breaking bread from house to house, did eat their meat with gladness and singleness of heart, Praising God, and having favour with all the people. And the Lord added to the church daily such as should be saved." (Acts 2:46-47)

Now, we somehow get the forty-seventh verse confused with the forty-first verse where the forty-first verse says, "Then they that gladly received his word were baptized: and the same day there were added unto them about three thousand souls." Now in the forty-seventh verse it says, "...Praising God, and having favour with all the people. And the Lord added to the Church daily such as should be saved." That should be noted, because it was added to them. They continued in the Apostles' doctrinal fellowship and added to them, which the apostles added to them, and their number became greater. But only God adds to the Church, He adds to the Church such as should be saved. We cannot determine who's saved, but if we can get them to fellowship with us, then God will save them when they become worthy to be saved.

I think we should slow down and refrain from our theory of addition to the doctrine of the apostles. Let us notice the condition of the time. I mean now. We have a problem with our spiritual life concerning the Church simply because we have prescribed and set our own standards and our own programs and function as an organization rather than an organism. We train people and program them in an unsound teaching and doctrine. We water down the soundness and truth of the Gospel of Jesus Christ, and we insert our own ideas, programs, lying, and substance of our teaching, which is unacceptable unto the Lord. People see the Church as an organization to be supported in a nonspiritual attitude, and all of our work representing the Church is church work. The time spent throughout the congregation is in doing church work and failing to do the works of the Church. Church work is not the function of salvation; it is the substance of ideas and material things. And notice that most times we place our progress upon the accomplishment of things. We measure our progress on the kind of building we build, the kind of progress we have, and by the beauty of our operation, such as luxurious interior, carpeting on the floor, carpeted pews, choir robes, ministers' robes, and jewelry on our fingers and hanging on our necks. This is where our enthusiasm comes from our progress.

The lost don't have a chance. They don't have a place in our functions. That's the works of the Church. We spend our time singing and supposedly worshipping among ourselves without any preparation for the supposed lost to be present, because in all of our preparation, we did nothing to get those in the midst of us in our worship services who have not accepted Christ. Our pride and attitude drives them away, because they feel they would be an embarrassment to be in our company or that we have already rejected them. Our outreach is poor. Our call to them to come and be a part is so cold and so uncertain there's no result of such things.

We spend our time at Church working with certain programs, such as an annual program. And something about people and congregations is that if they have one program and it works pretty well, it becomes an annual event. We make up our programs annually. We outline them, and tell the Lord this is what we are going to do. Now God is not a helping hand. God does not inspire that which He doesn't make. He is the maker. If you can make your program without God, why invite Him in to help you? I think the program should have God in the making. He makes the program, and then we have a reason to rely on Him for the success of the program. But we are caught up in our minds, our ability, and our desires to make our own programs. We hang it on the wall, on the calendar, and say, "Lord this is what we're going to do. Whether the time is acceptable, or you are in it, that's up to you, but this is the way we're going to do it." That's church work, measuring ourselves by finances or practicing gimmicks or sales, selling and buying to carry out our church work. This has to be an insult to the Holy Spirit, because God has provided the financial means for the operation of His Kingdom. He did that by working through those He required to establish tidings unto His Kingdom tidings and free will offerings. If they would submit themselves, and if we would do the proper teaching and training, they would summit themselves to give for not only extracurricular activities but to give offerings according to their prosperity. That certainly would be enough funds to operate the entire mission of which the Kingdom of God is made up and functions through what we know is the Church.

So, when we refrain from God's way, then we cannot succeed and be successful in the mission for which the work is meant. This mission is to save and to continue to build the Kingdom of God. You build that with souls. Remember, when man builds, he starts with a hammer and nails, mortar, and bricks, but when God builds, He builds alive. Whatever God builds, He builds life. Jesus said, "I will build my Church." He stressed heavily that the only way there would be action on the building was that if the person was born again. The only thing He builds is life. It lives. Whatever man builds, it builds up, and in time, it is brought down. But when God builds, life continues.

Our way is church work; it's not essential to salvation. It is not the answer to the fruits of the mission the Lord build in the hearts of men, which is the Kingdom of heaven to be built in the midst of earthly functions. There is no redemption. There is no spirit. There is no Holy Spirit in church work. It is in the works of the Church. Many people have gone through and are going through life doing their own assessment of themselves to be comfortable or satisfied that they are really the kind of people that the Lord has desired them to be in His purpose. If they feel like that person, then that's all it takes without noticing the fruits of their labor and recognizing that the fruits of the ministry are the lost. It is for the lost and to strengthen those believers or co-workers of the Lord Jesus. It's sad that we have strayed so long and so far without waking to the sense of becoming so rude to the physical world until it sounds silly. Many will frown on this information concerning the facts and the sound doctrine of the Kingdom of God. But believe it or not, like it or not, this is sound. This is the Word of God. This is unchangeable. We must recognize our shortcomings in our own lifestyles and realize our conduct and our attitudes are far from a spiritual expression. We can put on many forms of acts and become satisfied, but they are unacceptable and unspiritual. But, at the same time, we use it for the preparation of our eternity, which is not smart at all.

Let's notice the church work, how these one hundred and twenty developed into the function of the Kingdom of God. The Church was established not standing, but moving. No time was spent in the upper room after these believers received that promise. For a short time, when they began to settle down and realize what was happening, they realized they could no longer spend their time in the upper room, because every nation under the Heaven was not in the upper room but on the outside waiting to hear and waiting to become a part of this new covenant, this new Kingdom, that had been established and was ready to be exploded into a lost world. They hesitated and came out. They came out declaring to those outside their experience of what had happened on the inside. They didn't express their emotions and actions, they gave only what they had received, and that was the power of the Kingdom that had been established within them. Their work, which was the church work, was to make it clear that they were not able to join them in the upper room. There was no room. But there is room enough for all who comes He has already prepared room enough for you to come and join with us and add to our number and fellowship. The Lord will add you unto the Church, which is His kingdom.

This happened, and the number grew fast because many received, and they received only what was preached by those who had received the message. The works of the Church are the function of the Kingdom of God, which is the Church. It consists of preaching, teaching, witnessing, outreach, testifying, meditating, praising, and all that would make an addition to the positions that are carried out. It is not split up in pieces or bits. It is established into the hearts of all who receive it. Anyone who has been filled with the power of the Holy Ghost is a part of every function that goes on within the Church. A gift makes some more appropriate than others. There are gifts of singing, and those who can sing well cannot exclude those who cannot sing well. There are many that who are suited for taking part in the music because of their singing. That means there is room for all. Singing is for all separate, to sing. Prayer is not to be for those who just take on praying, but every person should feel the importance and the responsibility to carry out the function of the Church, not the part of the Church, but the function of the Church. You cannot carry out one part without carrying out the total function of the mission, the church work.

Church work has many departments, or many auxiliaries as we call them. We have someone to be responsible for every function of the church. We separate them, and they are only interested in that particular position into which you place them. But we turn the work of the Church into church work when we do not get the blessing of the Holy Spirit in church work. When we realize the function in us that was established by receiving Jesus Christ in our lives, we are just as responsible for one function as we are for the other. It is sad that choir members are not a part of the prayer service or that this auxiliary does not have a role in the other auxiliaries. But we have groups in many congregations, and the larger the congregation the larger the groups, and they all single out. You cannot have a church spread out. One accord means together. One accord means we not only meet together, we live together. Because the Church is not singled out into an individual. One individual cannot be the Church. One individual cannot represent the Kingdom of Heaven. It takes all functions. All.

In our automobile, one cylinder will not move and operate our automobile. Two cylinders won't do it. If it takes eight, only eight will do, whatever it takes for that automobile to run perfectly. If a machine must use its parts together to operate, how are we going to take the Church and split it up in parts, none working together? How can we do the works of the Lord? What happens to the engine when one stop? It misses. One miss, it's noticed. Two misses and there is a loss of power. Three misses, and it stops functioning all together, and it will not operate again until you get it fixed, and all cylinders are working together in harmony.

Here we have trustees or deacons. Trustees and deacons spend their lives confused with each other, because they are both claiming the same job. We have all kinds of boards and all degrees of usher boards. All single out everyone in their own vineyard, and they are unable to cooperate or function under the same Spirit, because they don't understand it. Furthermore, when you move from that oneness that establish the Kingdom in our hearts, you cannot operate.

So, these brethren followed the instructions of the Lord, the instruction of the Holy Spirit. For a long time the congregations lived and operated throughout the country under the soundness and function of the mother church in Jerusalem. Any group which practiced any other doctrine or any other plans different from what was brought out or sent out of the church of Jerusalem was unacceptable. All ministers preached the same doctrine, that which represented the New Testament Church.

Now we have as many splits of buildings and groups, and we have the splits in the mission of the Kingdom of Heaven. It is impossible for us to find the true meaning of the Kingdom of Heaven that has been established in our hearts. It is impossible for us to get an understanding and get a sense of ability as long as we try to operate under this nonsense, under this blindness that we're working with today. We must come back to this early Church and find ourselves spending our lives doing church work, and placing the works of the Church on hold.

We have lost, and we are still losing our younger generation simply because our programs and our ideas are not sufficient. They are not producing the kinds of seeds to plant in their lives for them to grow with the same fruit that produces church work or the *work of the church plant*. Church work has no seed; it is just something thrown together. It's artificial. But the work of the Church plants seeds. And it plants the same kind of seed, and brings forth the same kind of fruit.

Ministers, we must stop the kind of preaching we preach—the political stuff, the fancy stories. Let us preach what we are suppose to preach, the sound doctrine of Jesus Christ, so that we might establish and build His Kingdom in the lives of people—the believers and human beings. It was established to be built, with or without us. When this is completed, Jesus will come and receive it unto Himself. But I can't see Him receiving what we are calling ourselves and what we have set up while we are waiting on Him. If He will not visit us in the power of His Holy Spirit, certainly He's not coming to receive us if He doesn't visit us. He doesn't want us. He doesn't need us. If we can recognize Him as our leader in our life, in our spiritual life, and as our guide, our keeper, and our preserver, then we are convinced we are the people He will receive at His coming. But many of us have no spiritual evidence that we are His people, because we are producing nothing. We have no affect upon the lost. We have no plans to try to overcome the responsibility in which we have failed.

We are not getting any better. We're getting worse. We're filled with pride. We're trying to streamline and modernize something that shouldn't have been in the first place. So let the Church work. We are the Church, so let's do the work, the work of the Church. The work of Church is not the board of directors, the men who get their heads together and make up something. The Church is the body of Christ. His Holy Spirit is the life of the Church and is required in the building of the Kingdom, the function of the Church. We're dealing with lives, with people, and with communities, not with organizations, not with money making scams, and not with functions under the government.

The Church and the state are separated. The Lord built His Kingdom to not coincide with the kingdom of the Romans anyone else. He did not even discuss kingdomship with Israel, but He built His Kingdom in the heart of all those who would accept Him to move into their lives. It's not an Israelite. It's not a Jew. It's not a

Gentile. It's a believer. It's believing what He says and what He has done, and it is receiving Him into our lives in order to become the function of the Kingdom that He has built. This is what it's all about. This is what to preach. This is what to teach. This is what to live for. These brethren came down and spent their lives tincturing the Kingdom. You never find where Peter and the others decided to rest or to go on vacation. They labored in the building of the Kingdom to gain those who didn't understand. They preached and taught those concerning the Kingdom of God.

It is difficult to preach togetherness when you are not practicing being in one accord. I think the world should know it must come in our accord, not we coming in theirs. Come in our accord, because you are as much one as we are when you come in one accord.

So, it is God only who adds to the Church such as to be saved. He makes our numbers as one. Only He can make all numbers one no matters how many millions. He's the only one who can make them one. Therefore, He is the one who saves. He is the one who adds to the Church. He's the one who places the pieces of the building into his Kingdom. He didn't leave that to us. He left it to us to get their attention and to use our fellowship to bring them to be added with us. Yes, with us. The three thousand were added to them, to their fellowship, and added to their works. They added to their praise and added to their witnessing. And as they were added by numbers to them, the Lord added to the Church according to their true believers.

Every person who says he believes, doesn't believe, because he cannot believe. They cannot believe through the works of the Church. They cannot believe through church work. Only by the work of the Church can a person believe and know what to believe. Anyone can say, "I believe," but believe what? You ask them, "Do you believe on Jesus Christ?" "Yes, I believe, they say." What do you believe about Him? They say, "I believe that He exists because I hear others say He exists, but I have no personal experience to really be a witness." But if you say you believe and you can't witness, then that means that you don't believe. You have to have something to believe to be a witness. So, your congregations are filled with people who say that they believe, but they are not filled with witnessing.

Most of the people in your congregation are silent. They are speechless when they come together and congregate. They say nothing because they know nothing. They have nothing to say. They can't witness to what we are preaching. because they don't know what we're preaching. They are not in the mood to seek to learn what we preach. They can't even remember your text or what you preached about ten minutes after they are dismissed. We accept their word "believe through the years. Yes, they sit there saying they believe and never witness. You can't believe and not witness. If you believe, you are going to witness. That's what believing is all about. Believing is to witness. Believing is to serve. You don't believe and do nothing. You don't have to believe to do nothing. Just do nothing. So, believing is produced by the works of the Church, and when we fail to carry out the true mission and the function of the Church, then there is nothing to attract others to believe.

Those people just stood on the outside and noted the works of the Church, crying out, "What must we do? What can we do to be saved? What can we do to be a part of this?" They got the answer: believe on the Lord Jesus and be baptized in the name of the Lord Jesus Christ, and you begin there. That's how the number grew and how those people joined in. Those people who God added to the Church did not become persecutors later. No. Those people gave their lives. Those people maintained. Those people were the function of the Church, because they did the works of the Church. Those who were opposed to the spreading of the Church never became a part of it. They were never a part of those who stood around. They didn't inquire bout or seek a way to join themselves with the apostles and their doctrine. They were the ones who became opposed to the movement of the early Church.

So, everyone who believes becomes a witness, and witnesses do not stop witnessing to persecute the Church. Witnessing is what keeps us, occupies our time, and keeps us growing in the work. We understand that we are the ones who planted this in the minds of the people, and we are the ones to make known to them the difference between church work and the work of the Church. It is our responsibility, we are held responsible.

Amen, Amen.